T0287587

TITHE BARNS

JOSEPH ROGERS

AMBERLEY

First published 2021

Amberley Publishing
The Hill, Stroud,
Gloucestershire, GL5 4EP

www.amberley-books.com

Copyright © Joseph Rogers, 2021

The right of Joseph Rogers to be identified as the Author
of this work has been asserted in accordance with the
Copyrights, Designs and Patents Act 1988.

All rights reserved. No part of this book may be reprinted
or reproduced or utilised in any form or by any electronic,
mechanical or other means, now known or hereafter invented,
including photocopying and recording, or in any information
storage or retrieval system, without the permission in writing
from the Publishers.

ISBN: 978 1 4456 9285 2 (print)
ISBN: 978 1 4456 9286 9 (ebook)

British Library Cataloguing in Publication Data.
A catalogue record for this book is available from the British Library.

Typeset in 10pt on 13pt Celeste.
SJmagic DESIGN SERVICES, India.
Printed in the UK.

Contents

Introduction – Tithes and Tithing

During much of Britain's past, the concept we today know as tax was sourced by the unifying authority of the Church. With much of Britain's population working in agriculture, it was often this that formed the basis for the '*tithe*' – a tax consisting of one-tenth of a farmer's annual yield. Tithes were used to support the Church, aiding its abbeys or monasteries and any causes they saw fit to benefit from the proceeds. They were outlined for the Christian world in the Bible: '...bring all the tithes of that year's produce and store it in your towns...' (*Deuteronomy 14:22-29*). Tithes are thought to have been introduced to England by Saint Augustine, but also feature in other religions such as Islam and Sikhism.

Though tithing differed between territories in northern Europe, some taking cash or bonds and others sticking solely to agricultural produce, the system warranted a means to store items being brought to the relevant authority from its people. As a result, large

A 1946 serial publication from the USA contains propaganda promoting the payment of tithes. (Author's collection)

hollow structures of stone and timber, known as tithe barns, were erected. These allowed farmers to easily access a place to offer their tithe, while similarly giving the recipient a means to account for and siphon the produce.

The precise methods of using, collecting and accounting for tithes in Britain has been understood to varying degrees over many centuries, further complicated by differing religious authorities, events such as Henry VIII's dissolution of the monasteries, and the development of taxation beyond the authority of the Church. The Tithe Commutation Act of 1836 promoted the payment of tithes in cash instead of goods and prompted the drawing of tithe maps to determine who owned what land. It was not until 1966 that the tithe system in England officially ended altogether, and while today tithes are still offered to religious causes across the globe, this is often done on a voluntary basis.

In addition, the purpose of the tithe barn changed over time. These often large and secure structures saw use during times of strife and war before continuing into the present day in a variety of forms such as museums, hotels, public spaces and even private dwellings. Today, though there is much ambiguity over the history of many of the nation's tithe barns (such histories can be somewhat reclusive and inconspicuous), each offers a fascinating history of its local area and a tangible insight into how the present nation has been moulded by past events.

This title aims to present such insights by looking at the remaining barns spread across most parts of Britain. With tithing once the primary method of taxation, it is reasonable to assume that most parishes would have needed the use of a tithe barn at one point in the past, though it seems that the largest of the UK's towns and cities have destroyed physical evidence of them in their entirety. Of those left, it is immediately apparent that not all with the title 'tithe barn' were used to store tithes and therefore the hunt for genuine examples can be quite an undertaking. Some of the buildings mentioned here will be such imitators, with grange barns, abbey barns, estate barns and manorial barns frequently appearing among the truest examples. The history of, and construction techniques used in, all medieval barns have relevance to tithe-specific barns, though in each case it is hoped that the true designation and purpose can be highlighted where possible. Indeed over 500 results for the phrase 'tithe barn' exist in Historic England's Listed Building Register, and Cistercian monks are said to have built over 3,000 monastic barns in England alone. With many structures originating from the fourteenth, fifteenth and sixteenth centuries (and some from much earlier), it is no surprise that details of some have been lost to time. But, as is often the case in Britain, their very existence is something that the intrigued explorer can take time to appreciate during their travels.

1

Defining the Tithe Barn

Architecturally, all medieval barns have a fairly standard blueprint that allowed for the safe and secure storage of perishable crops before the days of meaningful refrigeration and complex preservatives. This included the need for thick walls, level foundations and adequate ventilation seen in the form of elongated slits at the gable ends of most examples. In addition, putlog holes featured to aid the construction of tall ceilings, offering the basis for basic scaffolding but also wooden floors that could be erected to stack produce higher and more efficiently. Flat and wide floors, particularly between porches, were more often than not threshing floors, which used the prevailing wind rolling in through the barn to separate grain from its chaff. The exposed nature of the interior allowed the draft to maintain freshness and birds to enter, keeping vermin levels to a minimum.

While the size of such structures by no means defined their use as a tithe barn, it is clear that some of the nation's larger examples were so because of the need to accumulate produce from many farmers at once. In some medieval barns, witches' marks and daisy wheels aided the preservation of crops by warding off the Devil, who would punish anyone withholding tithes. Some interpret such markings, particularly when accompanied with names and dates, as a way of recording tithe payments prior to tithe maps. While this would neatly tie up their meaning (and would definitively identify certain buildings as tithe barns), it is a theory without much credibility or proof.

The confusion between tithe barns and abbey barns is one that plagues the majority of examples in Britain and perhaps stems from some of the descriptive terms and phrases used in various records throughout time. Abbey barns were often similarly large and impressive buildings constructed within the grounds of abbeys and monasteries, or on land owned by them, and stored the produce farmed directly from their own land. As such yields already belonged to them, they were not considered tithes. On farms and in settlements away from the main establishment, referred to as outlying granges, grange barns held produce that again was owned directly by the abbey or monastery. While some examples may have interchangeably stored both produce offered as tithes and domestic produce, the distinction between the two processes is important to keep in mind and can easily cause confusion when learning more about medieval Britain.

When many of the great abbeys and monasteries were dissolved by Henry VIII in the 1530s, the right to receive tithes was sometimes passed on to those who were handed

Glastonbury Abbey ruins, Somerset. (Author's collection)

swathes of property by the newly created, self-professed head of the Church of England. Other tithing rights simply transferred to the Anglican Church. Despite, in some cases, this right losing its ecclesiastical connection, tithe barns were no less important, or relevant.

The result today is that the terms are often used rather loosely (even the most reputable authorities such as Historic England, the National Trust and Ordnance Survey use them interchangeably) and smaller trusts and owners have sometimes been misled one way or another over the purpose of their ageing barn over time. As historians delve deeper into archives and records, occasionally hastily named barns are revised to simply 'Great Barn' or 'Medieval Barn', which portrays meaningful importance for visitors, clients and inhabitants alike without reducing such structures to the same level as other more generic agricultural buildings.

2

Scotland and Northern England

The search for Britain's tithe barns begins with a glance at the remaining examples in Scotland. Unlike England's southern reaches, which are peppered heavily with such buildings, Scotland has only a few examples left standing. Exactly how many is hard to say definitively, particularly when noting that the word 'teind' has been used in these parts to describe tithes and it is unknown how many might have been built to begin with. Historic Environment Scotland records two remaining structures, though other sources cite a third in the Shetland Isles and another once stood in Linlithgow, West Lothian. Whatever the actual figure, the lack of Roman and Christian influences in the Highlands is perhaps why these two barns are located near the present-day border with England.

The village of Foulden lies a mere mile into Scottish territory and is known for its neat and distinctive row of cottage buildings and for the small kirk which, in 1587, held a meeting between commissioners over the execution of Mary Queen of Scots. Its tithe barn, located within the churchyard, is typical of others as its construction date is unknown (possibly seventeenth century) and its ability to store tithes is uncertain. Alterations were made in the 1700s and 1800s in line with other structural changes to its surroundings, though it is noted for having largely intact interior wooden beams. At one point it was used as a grain store, a popular form of tithe throughout Britain.

Further north, more ambiguity arises from the existence of a similarly shaped building at Whitekirk, near North Berwick. Once an important site of pilgrimage, the village has a significant religious past and in the fifteenth century it hosted Enea Silvio Bartolomeo Piccolomini, the future Pope Pius II, following his treacherous voyage from Italy to Dunbar. Such was the draw of the village and its celebrated holy well that hostels were built to house pilgrims making offerings to the Blessed Virgin Mary. The tithe barn, overlooking the village church from the north, may have been constructed from the remains of such hostels as demand dropped away following the development of the village and loss of the well. Despite the resemblance to other tithe barns, including the one at Foulden, it has been suggested that the building did not originally store tithes and was instead part of a tower built in the sixteenth century by Oliver Sinclair, only becoming a tithe barn for the village in the seventeenth century. Other sources within the village suggest Abbot Crawford of Holyrood might have occupied the building prior to that. Nineteenth-century maps name the building 'The Granary' and also pinpoint the 'supposed site' of the holy well

Foulden Teind Barn, Scotland is currently used to store grounds-keeping equipment and masonry. (Author, with kind permission of Historic Environment Scotland)

some 200 metres east. Fittingly, the building remains in private ownership having been refurbished in the 1990s and currently offers accommodation to holidaymakers.

It is in England, however, where the presence of tithe barns can be felt strongest and upon trekking south from Scotland through present-day Cumbria, Northumberland and County Durham, they can appear in some rather unexpected places.

This begins with a look at England's northernmost city, Carlisle, which hosts an attractive array of sandstone buildings at the historic quarter in and around the Cathedral. Among these is the fifteenth-century tithe barn on the corner of West Walls and Head Lane. Unusually, this barn seems to have been open to the elements on the north side until its restoration in 1971 when it was enclosed and used as a community hall. Previously it had seen use as the Carlisle Dispensary, stables and a joiner's shop, and is depicted with a gently smoking chimney in an 1895 painting by Thomas Bushby. Despite its survival resulting from efforts made by the adjacent St Cuthbert's Church, who are also now responsible for its use and upkeep, the barn would have been part of the Augustinian Priory of St Mary, which had commanding views to the south owing to the fortified nature of the city's centre. The thickness of the wall running parallel to Heads Lane is made clearer by its contrast with the new concrete gable end, which acts as a necessary feature to keep alive a rare example of such a barn in an urban setting.

The Rectory, Grasmere. The former tithe barn is the annex to the left of the picture. (Author)

Conversely, finding the small tithe barn in the village of Grasmere, at the heart of the Lake District National Park, provides something of a challenge to those unfamiliar with the building's appearance. It is pinned obscurely onto the large rectory opposite St Oswald's Church that was occupied briefly by poet William Wordsworth as he hopped between a number of properties in Grasmere during the early 1800s. The tithe barn became a community hall after funding from the church, who then put it up for sale with the rectory in 2018, raising some eyebrows among the locals who have since questioned whether funds from the sale would remain 'in the village'. Coincidentally, such questions were raised in the past by villagers up and down the country about the use of tithes by the Church, sometimes causing friction. This was certainly the case for the medieval 'middle class' who lived on the edge of poverty without assistance from the Church while still being taxed a tenth of their farmed produce.

The future of Grasmere's tithe barn within its new private setting remains unclear, though its sale listing remarked that local authorities would support a change of use and suggest that it would make for an ideal snooker room, gym or granny flat – a far cry from its original purpose.

One of the more unusual places to find a barn in present-day England is on the periphery of a major prison complex. This is the case in Durham, where a fifteenth-century granary, complete with aged timbers and crumbling masonry, sits perched on the end of the Prison Officers' Club on Hallgarth Street. Built in 1424, it likely stored grain as part of the farm at Durham Priory, and featured a large barn beside it, since heavily altered. Historic England refers to its tithe barn title as 'erroneous' and since 1540, when the priory was dissolved, the building has seen Durham's city centre rise around it, including Her Majesty's Prison Durham in 1819. Almost two centuries later, it was opened as an 'invitation only' museum displaying curios from the world of crime and shed light on the imprisonment of Myra Hindley, Ian Brady and Ronnie Kray. Today, however, the newly named Tythe Barn Club looks tired despite continued use as a function room and, while being Grade II listed, it is also on the Heritage At Risk register.

The general absence of remaining tithe barns in the north of England means that where one might exist, others may appear in its vicinity. Indeed, this would seem to be the case in one part of Yorkshire where a small collection of notable barns have remained in one form or another.

Tythe Barn Club, Durham. This old granary has since seen many different uses. (Author)

North-west of York city centre are the ancient settlements of Upper Poppleton and Nether Poppleton. The latter hosts a large number of former agricultural buildings surrounding Manor Farm, including a brick-built tithe barn next to the church of St Everilda. The story surrounding the tithe barn's present use and survival is one married to that of the local community's desire to see the legacy of village life maintained in the area. A huge amount of pride, abundant across Yorkshire, saw the formation of Poppleton Preservation Group (PPG) in 1989 to highlight the importance of the area and the tithe barn at Manor Farm was marked for redevelopment that year. The results depict a building whose history arguably defines that of Nether Poppleton itself.

Dendrochronological testing by Sheffield University from within the building revealed origins from 1542/1543, but more importantly suggested that the wood was not reused timber and so was felled with the building of the tithe barn in mind. This date ties in well with the change of ownership of the land following the dissolution of the religious houses. Crucially, research by PPG also shed light on the tithe payments made and, while the barn might not have existed until after the dissolution of St Mary's Abbey in York, who had owned the area, the land and tithes were likely inherited by the Archbishop of York, thus warranting a place to store produce for this purpose. During the Hutton family's residence at Manor Farm from 1590, it is again suggested that the barn housed tithes.

The tithe barn's place in national history was cemented on 1 July 1644 when, during the Civil War, Prince Rupert was reputed to have held troops in the barn prior to his crossing of the River Ouse and progressing to the Battle of Marston Moor the following day. In time some locals would come to refer to the barn as Rupert's Barn.

At this point its exterior would have looked different from its present state. It may have then been more similar to what we now call a Dutch Barn. Over the centuries alterations were made to it and the local brick casing surrounding the barn was implemented in the eighteenth century once the tithes became cash payments and it became a threshing barn. Now, only 40 per cent of the barn remains following a fire in 1928 and the brick exterior also features a thick, solitary buttress on its south side.

In 1989, the retirement of the Manor Farm tenant farmer gave the owner, North Yorkshire County Council, the opportunity for residential development – they saw the tithe barn's redundancy. Until then, for many years, the farmer had used it for storage. A substantial effort by locals to avoid its conversion into two private dwellings was successful and prompted its use as a venue for weddings, meetings and other communal uses. This process itself garnered some level of fame for the village with the fundraising and subsequent restoration being recognised by Prince Andrew, Duke of York in 1999 and the area's wider historical significance bringing Channel 4's *Time Team* to Nether Poppleton (with the tithe barn hosting the incident room) in 2004.

Today, a dedicated group of trustees (of the Friends of Nether Poppleton Tithe Barn charitable trust), some of whom were at the forefront of ensuring the barn's survival, gladly share details of its past and manage bookings for its use. It is clear that their approach and liaison with the authorities was firm and cooperative and saw both North Yorkshire County Council and the Heritage Lottery Fund buy into the idea that the tithe barn be a lasting example of Nether Poppleton's rural history.

Above and overleaf: Nether Poppleton Tithe Barn interior, before and after. (Nether Poppleton Tithe Barn Trustees)

14

This wall is all that remains of the tithe barn in Selby. (Author)

South of York, remains of former tithe barns exist at both Bolton Percy (now a scheduled ancient monument) and at Selby, which has an impressive abbey at its centre. Sadly, all that is left of Selby's tithe barn is a small section of wall reclaimed from its demolition during the nineteenth and twentieth centuries, which was incorporated into the Abbey Vaults pub in 1982. The vacant area of land now hosts a car park where the barn once stood and its dimensions, some 313 feet by 23 feet, are displayed on a plaque nearby.

Heading west and close to Leeds' periphery is the linear village of Aberford. Some unusual characteristics feature in the settlement's architecture, including the striking Gascoigne Almshouses to its south and the local church's dedication to St Ricarius, who supposedly visited in 630. The tithe barn now houses the Church of England Primary School and is owned by the Archdeacon of York following its transfer from the Vicar of Aberford. Previously, it and much of the village was owned by Oriel College, Oxford, which also received tithes from Aberford. Evidence of this is found in local parish records, which contain a 'copy of certain tithes sent to Oriel College ... 1790–1799' paid in rapeseed, turnips and lamb.

The format of tithes largely mirrored that of the rest Britain but one unusual form of rent payment from Penistone (to whom, it is unknown) was that of a red rose at Christmas time and a snowball during summer. Here a snowball may have been a Guelder-rose and though not documented as clearly as other produce, it demonstrates the importance that herbs and flowers had as commodities for healing and decoration.

At Bolton Abbey near Skipton, the sixteenth-century barn, some 55 metres in length, has gone from being a relatively unknown landmark among the ruins of the former priory to a high-profile showpiece of Pearce Bottomley Architects, who extensively modernised the

Above and opposite: Work on Bolton Abbey Tithe Barn received glowing praise from RIBA, who awarded it their Yorkshire Conservation Award for 2019. (Tom Robbins)

Tithe Barn Cottage, Whittington, Lancashire – now two separate dwellings. (Author)

barn to form an event space for the estate in 2018, being recognised by RIBA in the process. The position of the porches and incredible length single it out among others in Yorkshire.

To the west, Lancashire provides much in the way of locations once proud of their now-vanished tithe barns as well as a small number of existing ones. At Whittington, in the Lune Valley, the former tithe barn now fronts Main Street and is very much part of the village vernacular with grey stonework and uniform windows on one gable end indicative of its present life as two private dwellings. Little is known about its history as a barn, though the property's omission from the 1911 census has led locals to suggest that it may still have been a barn around that time. Since then, a number of villagers have lived in the barn and it was worked on significantly during the twenty-first century. Today one half is let to holidaymakers. A building under the name of 'tithe barn' similar in size and proportions exists at Arkholme nearby, now a five-bedroom private dwelling.

Further south, within the clutches of the Forest of Bowland, lies Browsholme Hall (pronounced 'Bru-som'), which claims to be the county's oldest surviving family home. The grand house has been added to, amended and restored over the last 500 years largely under the supervision of the Parker family, whose current members preside over their house partly as a heritage landmark.

The tithe barn within the grounds is thought to date from the eighteenth century and is joined by other outbuildings within a refurbished courtyard area. Inside the barn, there are curved queen post trusses and its exterior hosts an unusually large number of doors. One big enough for carts sits in the north-east corner of the building and the largest are those that link it with the rest of the complex at one gable end. Elsewhere these entrances, low in height and narrow in width, have been sealed and the globular finials at each corner of the roof seem to be recent additions. Despite a fire in the nineteenth century, the barn remained in use on the farm until 2008 when dairy operations moved to more modern facilities on site. At this point the barn was converted into its current guise serving fine afternoon tea and welcoming guests and visitors. As a wedding venue, the barn has won a number of awards, in addition to the estate's Forest of Bowland 'Sustainable Tourism Award'. Little evidence exists around the payment of tithes as produce from the area and the barn was likely used primarily for the storage of produce for the estate.

Serving refreshments of a different kind is the tithe barn at Garstang which has been host to one of the town's pubs under the name Th'Owd Tithe Barn overlooking the nearby Lancaster Canal. Dating from 1701, the barn pre-dates the canal by almost 100 years and gives name to the alternatively spelled Tythe Barn Moorings. The barn would have been used to store corn before being converted into a public house. The current layout of the pub is largely down to work carried out in 1973 and today the exterior distinguishes various elements of the building with white rendering and bare stone walls in addition to utilitarian extracting pipes and barrel stores.

When approaching the built-up landscape of Preston, not much of it exudes agriculture and it is perhaps reasonable to assume that in the modern age, evidence of a tithe barn in the area is scarce. However, today's Preston is arguably defined by the legacy of its tithe barn and the failure of a stillborn scheme to revolutionise the city with a large retail area.

The Tithebarn Regeneration Project initially began with proposals made in 2005 and saw the city council partner with international property groups to plan Preston's transformation. The location of the scheme took its name from the building formerly on Old Vicarge (since demolished) that also lent its title to the Tithebarn Hotel and Tithebarn Street. This street now hosts the Grade II listed brutalist bus station, threatened with removal under the same redevelopment plans. Ultimately, these plans were rejected by other councils and the project cancelled in 2011, saving the bus station that has since become one of Preston's defining landmarks.

The combination of localised politics and the existence of a past tithe barn also makes its mark on nearby Poulton-le-Flyde, in the form of the Tithebarn electoral ward. Tithebarn Street and Tithebarn Place also exist in the town, though the origins of the barn itself are elusive.

A brief mention of the Isle of Man, a short hop westward from England's north-west coast, is relevant as a number of sources highlight the historical importance of tithes and the influence that the twelfth-century Rushen Abbey had on the island. As with some coastal settlements in England, Manx tithes were sometimes paid in fish and it is known that tithe barns once existed on the island for the storage of hemp and pulse. Other produce such as cattle and corn were farmed over various centuries but were also moved between Ireland and Scotland as trade became as important as mining or fishing.

Naturally, trade also saw the rise and success of the city of Liverpool and surrounding communities on the River Mersey but, unlike major cities further south, did little to quash the importance of tithes. Like Preston, a large legacy is left by the barn that once stood on one corner of Cheapside where it meets the main road, now an area saturated with commercial offices. The right to receive tithes in Liverpool and nearby Kirkdale was originally held by Shrewsbury Abbey before being purchased by the Molyneux family.

Above and below: Preston Tithe Barn, from which the hotel and street are named, is shown here in 1937 (above) and the 1960s (below) next to Cardwell's Brewery. Both buildings no longer exist. (Images courtesy of Lancashire County Council's Red Rose Collections)

Sir William Molyneux erected the tithe barn in *c.* 1524 and it remained for many centuries as the city centre grew up around it. Changing times saw the building being converted into shops and it is thought to have been taken down sometime after 1820, though some sources indicate that it may still have been present, albeit altered, as late as the 1900s.

It is no surprise therefore to see that the building became enough of a local landmark to name the main thoroughfare on which it stood: 'Tithebarn Street'. Major businesses and organisations today also take the name 'Tithebarn', often formed as one word, for locations and offices along the street. Liverpool John Moores University has the infamous *Superlambanana* placed outside its Tithebarn Building not far from where the barn once stood, and the seven-storey office block on the corner of Old Hall Street now takes the name No. 1 Tithebarn following a refurbishment in 2008 to update its 1980s image.

This theme of keeping the tithe barn name alive spreads out to places such as Knowsley, where a tithe barn from 1720 used to exist on what is now Tithebarn Road. At Cantril Farm, a centre of notorious violence and unemployment during the 1980s, the local pub The Tithebarn also passed its name onto the local Sunday League football team 'Tithebarn

Right and overleaf: Liverpool's Old Tithe Barn *c.* 1800 – now immortalised by Tithebarn Street. (Author's collection/ Author)

FC'. After the area split its ownership in 1983, part of the estate was renamed Stockbridge Village and both the pub and team adopted the name The Village as a result.

In Melling, just north of Great Crosby where a care home also takes on the tithe barn name, the former tithe barn still remains thanks to the efforts of the local vicar and villagers in the 1970s. The building, no longer needed by the farm of which it was a part, is now frequently used by locals for arts sessions, dancing lessons and personal occasions and seems to have been modified to suit its present use with a small extension and chimney where the cart entrance would once have been. On the chimney's exterior, the date 1826 is inscribed, leading some sources to quote this as the construction date, but this seems far too late for the erection of a tithe barn, given that almost all tithes were commuted to cash ten years later.

Records show that tithe barns existed in the towns of Litherland and Maghull as well as Lunt, which has since had its seventeenth-century barn converted into homes. What the north lacks in the way of medieval examples tied inextricably to abbeys, as in the south, it more than makes up for with significant references to the tithing concept.

While such references around Merseyside all lie within a short distance of Liverpool's centre, any similar appearances in the Greater Manchester area are spread further to outlying settlements with the closest reference being at Clayton Hall where a former barn once stood.

At Stockport, the local school takes on the name Tithe Barn Primary after being established as an open-air school in 1929, though the current building dates from 1970. Nearby, Tithe Barn Cottage and Tithe Barn Road hint at such a barn being prominent in the town.

In Radcliffe, an MOT centre takes its unlikely place within the structure of the former tithe barn, nestled within a row of terraced housing and near to the site of Radcliffe Manor, with which it may have had an association. The ruins of Radcliffe Tower, just around the corner from the barn, may have provided some of the sandstone used in its construction sometime in the seventeenth or eighteenth century, and though the barn is quite small compared to others, the inclusion of bee holes, a hay loft and cattle dock indicate that it saw a variety of local produce stored within. Its location on Tithebarn Street, not far from St Mary's Church, does nothing to stem the flow of suspicion surrounding its tithe barn status, at least according to adjacent notice boards.

Understanding the importance of their place of work, the staff at B&G MOT Centre take pride in operating under the original wooden beams and in many ways its continued use for something so far beyond the technological means of those who built it becomes oddly satisfying. Crucially, it keeps the barn intact and looked after, making the addition of security gates, an advertising board and a solid, flat floor, necessary sacrifices.

Radcliffe Tithe Barn is now used as a local MOT centre. (Author)

3

Wales and the Midlands

Unlike Scotland, the concept of paying tithes in kind was just as well known in Wales as it was in England and, as a result, tithe barns were certainly required on land defined by its farming ways. Oddly, perhaps due to the isolation of farms within the valleys, finding remaining barns used for tithing seems to be quite difficult, even when using the Welsh term *Ysgubor Ddegwm*.

A small number of these make themselves known through some form of self-catered luxury accommodation tapping into outdoor pursuit holidays in the glorious landscapes around Snowdonia or the Brecon Beacons. Abercelyn House, fronting the beautiful Llyn Tegid, utilises its tithe barn in this way, giving its occupants a cosy setting from which to explore the surrounding area. The former barn is thought to date from around 1729 and likely stored tithes on behalf of the rector in connection with St Beuno's Church opposite.

It is in South Wales, though, where sparsely spread tithe barns are made use of more publicly. Though Cwmbran is most certainly a New Town with little to offer in the way of an extensive past, the land on which it is built was once part of the wider Llantarnam Abbey grounds. Today, the former Cistercian Abbey hosts the Sisters of St Joseph and while it is now enclosed by passing A-roads, suburban housing and industrial estates, the barn remains, albeit ruined, behind the main building. Its current state may have resulted from its 'despoiling' in 1836, coincidentally the year in which tithes were commuted to cash payment.

The survival of Abergavenny's tithe barn could not be more of a contrast, sitting proudly at the centre of the town alongside St Mary's Priory, whose tithe payments it would have stored until the dissolution. After this, its use was varied and its calling became one of entertainment, including a seventeenth-century theatre and a disco in the 1900s – in addition to various guises as a carpet warehouse, shop, food hall and auction house.

The barn's form, which probably dates from the sixteenth century (though it may originate from the twelfth century), eventually required extensive restoration. This began in 2002 and resulted in its current unique appearance. Gentle curves bulge from the western wall beneath a renewed tiled roof and though the uniform pigeon holes have been plugged, their confinement to the upper part of the east side complement the unusual but attractive circular windows. In 2008, it was appropriately opened by His Royal Highness

Llantarnam Abbey Barn. Wire fencing and intrusive fauna do little to celebrate the ruins of this rare Welsh barn. (Author, with kind permission of The Sisters of St Joseph of Annecy)

the Prince of Wales, whose name now graces the adjacent courtyard. The prominence and utilisation of the barn today makes it arguably the most important tithe barn in Wales.

Perhaps its only competitor is found within Brecon. Here the tithe barn has been chopped and changed since its possible use storing tithe hay for the adjacent priory in the 1500s, and is thought to have been longer than its current footprint suggests. Most of its exterior dates from later in the seventeenth century and incorporates the boundary wall of what is now Brecon Cathedral. The last century saw its conversion to a heritage centre, shop and café, shedding light on the priory's far-reaching past.

Elsewhere, barns crop up in isolated hamlets and villages near Ross-on-Wye and Llangolen with another, now a theatre, facing Exmoor across the Bristol Channel at St Donats on the south coast. In line with the rest of western Britain they are all of a stone exterior, with wood confined to the beams and trusses inside.

Heading east, Wales gives way to England though a complex to-ing and fro-ing of the present-day boundary. At the border with Shropshire between Newtown and Lydham, motorists could be forgiven for feeling confused as they drive into England, then back into Wales, then back into England once again. Shropshire's lands act as something of a rural middle-ground between the rising mountains and valleys of Powys and the industrialised Black Country. As a result the area is rife with historic manors, settlements and agricultural buildings.

The isolation of some of these estates and villages is perhaps best demonstrated by Upton Cressett, a location only accessible by going off the beaten track. What seems like an endless gearbox battle by car eventually results in a dead end at Upton Cressett Hall,

Above and below: Abergavenny and Brecon Tithe Barns. Though few in number, remaining barns in Wales are utilised well. The appearance of the one at Abergavenny is unique in Britain. (Author)

an impressive fifteenth-century house modified extensively in the sixteenth-century by the High Sheriff of Shropshire, Richard Cressett. Of more interest is the 900-year-old Church of St Michael below it, now redundant and in the care of the Churches Conservation Trust. In the 1850s, Eyton's *Antiquities of Shropshire* dissected the village and its history, coming across some difficulty with the identity of Upton (or Ulton/Ultone) near Stottesdon and tithes paid with respect to Salop Abbey during Stephen's reign of England in the twelfth century. Assuming the likely connection between this Upton and Upton Cressett to be true, the remaining barn within the grounds of the hall may well have stored these tithes. Sadly, little more can be determined about the barn's past but its present is defined by a significant conversion into a reclusive home among other equally reclusive buildings owned by Sir William Cash MP.

The nearby village of Stanton Long sheds a little more light on the construction of its Tithe House, facing the roadside up from the church. Its Grade II listing from 1954 consists only of two sentences but at least estimates its erection in the seventeenth century and highlights the obvious wood panelling that clads one part of the otherwise brick-built exterior. It is frequently referred to as the tithe barn and records show that tithes from Stanton Long were at one time acquired by Wenlock Priory, though some 400 years prior to this barn's existence.

Perhaps the most important medieval barn in Shropshire (and some might argue, the country) is what remains of the example at Acton Burnell Castle, built in the thirteenth century by Robert Burnell. Significant lands were given to Burnell by Prince Edward (later King Edward I) as the result of a close friendship, which in turn saw his rise to chancellor of England and Bishop of Bath and Wells thereafter. His right to use royal woodland for timber saw the construction of an impressive manor and outbuildings as well as the nearby church. Burnell's heavy political involvement saw this manor host what is considered the first meeting of parliament in England, which took place in the nearby tithe barn in c. 1285, headed by Edward I and consisting of both nobles and commoners.

The castle subsequently passed through the ownership of a number of families and was taken in 1487 by King Henry VII after the War of the Roses. During the 1600s and 1700s the grounds were used by the village for recreation with the barn decaying to only its gable ends. Bizarrely, the barn's parliamentary significance is somewhat lost on what is now an openly accessible English Heritage landmark. The remains of Parliament Barn are actually within the grounds of Concord College and not accessible to the public, but even so references outside of Shropshire to England's first convening of parliament are surprisingly modest.

Such modesty would do no favours, however, to the seventeenth-century tithe barn at Norton on the busy A442 between Telford and Bridgnorth. It is used today as a premier wedding venue and sees its presence candidly advertised in and around the West Midlands. An array of celebratory options are offered by the Hundred House Hotel, itself a fine building, utilising the barn's original timbers and footprint as well as considerate comforts in the bar and mezzanine floor. It is thought that this barn was constructed to replace the separately listed fifteenth-century courthouse barn opposite, arguably more attractive with its contrasting white walls and dark timber. Collectively, all three buildings create a setting spanning up to 500 years of history, which is perhaps why the tithe barn was voted Best Wedding Venue in the West Midlands in both 2018 and 2019.

Many prospective couples no doubt have origins in the nearby Black Country, today a melting pot for materialistic retail and refreshing multiculturalism, rather than the Victorian coal mining, iron-forging and glass-blowing which gave the area its name. Here, tithes were effectively phased out during the eighteenth century as much of the land

Acton Burnell Castle. The famous barn, an ageing ruin even as early as 1796, is seen to the right of this illustration. (Author's collection)

previously used for farming was dug up, made barren and industrialised to make way for coal mines. This had quite an impact on those entitled to tithes and as E.J. Evans explains in a 1970 report for the *Agricultural History Review*, titled 'Tithing Customs and Disputes: the Evidence of Glebe Terriers, 1698 – 1850', a certain Edward Eginton, Vicar of Wednesbury in 1730, lost much of his profitable land to the town's extensive mining operations. As a result, it is not surprising to see that remaining tithe barns in this part of the Midlands are hard to come by – in fact, they're arguably non-existent.

However, Evans's report also sheds light on the rigorous record keeping of tithe payments in Staffordshire (which included most of the present-day Black Country until 1974) by way of glebe terriers – documents surveying land and property. In Tixall, near Stafford, a comprehensive breakdown of commodities subject to tithing is laid out for the year 1698 and includes livestock in the form of cows (and separately calves), sheep (with tithes sometimes offered in fleeces), pigs, geese, and chickens (similarly in eggs), as well as honey and apples. Offerings were referred to as 'tythe piggs', 'tythe honey' and so on and where farmers had not enough produce to easily offer one-tenth, those taking tithes would sometimes take 'half-tythes' (though this was not common nationally) or carry over the tithe into the following year.

Worcestershire, at the southern reaches of the West Midlands, has a small collection of villages bordering the Cotswolds and Gloucestershire that have noteworthy barns and tithes were certainly contested here in the 1800s, causing the dispute that resulted in the Oddesley murders of 1806. Two of these barns, at Middle Littleton and Bredon, are now owned by the National Trust, the former with origins as early as 1250 closing in on Britain's oldest examples. Connected to Evesham Abbey, it made use of the surrounding orchards to store tithes as apples, though it is likely that such a barn would have stored

A servant is serving a tithe pig on a plate to the Rector sitting at the table. (W. Holland, 1791, Wellcome Collection CC BY)

bulkier tithes in hay and grain to warrant a building of its size. On the other side of Evesham, to the south, maps show a tithe barn isolated in a field bordering a new housing development off the A46 and aerial photos show it to be ruined. The age, purpose and history of this barn are not known.

The Bredon Barn, slowly and correctly moving away from the tithe barn moniker and built around 1350, was likely a manorial barn and its past confusion with tithe barns almost certainly results from its size, style and connection with the Bishop of Worcester. Throughout the year crops ranging from wheat and barley (used for brewing) to wool and hay would have been stacked high in the barn, with excess being transported to Tewkesbury for sale. Grain stored in the barn was the yield from approximately 150 acres of land and therefore required a large space for mass storage. Rumour suggests the barn may have been used by Shakespeare as a theatre while on tour, giving this example an under-appreciated celebrity status. In 1980, the storage of hay fed a catastrophic fire, which resulted in a three-year restoration project using the same Cotswold stone and oak to patch and repair the roof. Some of the original timbers survived this ordeal.

Bredon Barn. Despite the fire and restoration work, little has changed since this photograph was taken in the early 1900s. (Author's collection)

The same could not be said for the barn recorded at Ashton under Hill, which was totally gutted by fire in 1940 despite the documented punctuality of Evesham Fire Brigade. The same fate befell the seventeenth-century example in Kidderminster some twenty years later, though this time the fire brigade were prevented from saving the barn by poorly parked cars blocking the roads around it.

At Polesworth, Staffordshire, where the West and East Midlands collide, a seventeenth-century tithe barn sits back from the high street not far from where Polesworth Abbey would have stood prior to 1536. Though the two are not likely linked due to the age gap, the existence of Polesworth Hall and St Editha's Church may have seen the need to store tithes in the barn. Little exists beyond this speculation to determine whether or not its title is legitimate and in fact its Grade II listing refers to it as the Tame Barn, presumably in connection with nearby Tamworth's water course, the River Tame. Oddly, it is the Anker, a tributary of the Tame, that flows through Polesworth.

The counties of Leicestershire and Northamptonshire contain the most notable examples in the East Midlands region, with the extreme east offering a rather barren area for prospective research. The famous Bosworth battlefield now makes much of its barn as part of a tourism venture in the form of the 1485 Tithe Barn Café. Anecdotes from other tithe barn owners and historians judge this particular example as how not to sympathetically restore such an old building, but such is the subjective nature of medieval barn conversions. The fact that it still stands is commendable.

Above and overleaf: Cosby Tithe Barn. Original wattle and daub (pictured) exposed during restoration is now displayed behind glass for diners. The tasteful setting brings the barn into use and is admired by its new audience. (The Tithe Barn, Cosby)

Conversion to an upmarket dining experience also became the fate of the second-oldest building in Cosby, south-west of Leicester. This time however, much consideration has gone into keeping alive the history of the building, even down to the staff being knowledgeable and enthusiastic about the setting in which they serve their customers. Dating from the fifteenth century, the barn was likely linked to Leicester Abbey as one of its granaries before being absorbed into a village farm thereafter. In the 1960s a local haulage company, H.W. Coates, took over the barn with the rest of the site making way for their base of operations. Later in the 1980s, the decaying structure was saved, albeit as commercial office space. The barn's transformation into a compact but comfortably rustic setting for diners came through Marriott Group Ltd, who seized the opportunity when the haulage yard became luxury housing in what is now an attractive commuter village for Leicester. With renewed thatch and restored woodwork, the tithe barn's current use is both a modernisation and a celebration of the structure, allowing those socialising over a garnished sandwich or rich coffee to do so while appreciating the quality and history of the building.

4

Into England's East

Heading further east, and into Bedfordshire, references appear to tithe barns that fell victim to the post-war development of outlying villages and farms into suburban districts of major towns. Houghton Regis, near Luton, now has the Bedford Square shopping centre gracing the location of what was Tithe Farm behind All Saints Church. The wooden-clad barn, along with the farm, was wiped out in 1964, highlighting the redundancy of the tithe barn concept and prioritisation of growth in modern Britain. The same fate befell Wootton's tithe barn, south-west of Bedford, in 1955, presumably for the residential development now bearing Tithe Barn Road.

Newnham Priory, closer to Bedford's town centre, succumbed to dissolution well before this in 1540, but the associated Fenlake Barns nearby were saved under ownership of the Crown before going through private hands between 1599 and 1987, including Trinity College Cambridge between 1890 and 1940. The tithe barn, now part of The Barns Hotel, has perhaps some of the best-preserved woodwork of any barn in the UK and those now looking to utilise it as a wedding or conference venue would have to look hard to find any replacement beams. In the south of England, the story of old ships being broken up and recycled into structures such as tithe barns is common, but in this barn evidence of rigging holes in the larger wooden posts evidence this theory. Internal sources from the hotel's parent company suggest origins in the thirteenth century, though Historic England cites construction some 300 years later. While the barn in this part of Bedford survived any extensive changes in the built environment, it did become part of a wartime scheme to store the belongings of people whose houses had been bombed during the Second World War and in later years became a store for boats.

Cambridgeshire preserves its notable structures more sympathetically, exporting British heritage to the world through institutions like Cambridge University. It therefore keeps its selection of ageing barns to a high standard. In addition, a transition is made somewhere between the mostly stone structures in the west and the wooden ones of the east which, it has been argued, was not only a difference in construction methods and periods (for example a lack of stone from which to quarry or abundance of timber), but also a significant indicator of power and wealth among abbeys and parishes. Such establishments that were able to build grand, permanent stone barns likely did so to exercise their power. Smaller, wooden barns, on the other hand, were easily erected and taken down in line with the changing ownership of lands and tithes.

Manor Farm in Bourn now forms a small retail setting from its refurbished outbuildings with a wooden, jet black barn as the centrepiece. Its colour, size and angular features resemble something from the fictitious Empire in *Star Wars* – and at up to 700 years old it was indeed built 'a long time ago'. A previous house and tithe barn existed on the site prior to 1266, but it was razed to the ground by supporters of Simon De Montfort following the Battle of Evesham a year earlier and the current barn is thought to have been built after this. The Great Barn now uses its spacious interior for everything from photo shoots and weddings to Christmas fares and community events, with the rest of the farm hosting a café, hair salon and butcher's shop.

At Landbeach, north of Cambridge, substantial restoration efforts on its barn have been recently completed following delivery of a sizeable grant from the National Lottery Heritage Fund to supplement other fundraising efforts. As something of an emblem in the village, featured along with the church on the sign at its centre, it has significant support via the Tithe Barn Trust, who wish to ensure the survival and use of the barn, which is thought to date from at least 1549. Its historical ties with the rectory and its rectors shed uncertainty over exact dating but references to a tithe barn in the village existed as early as 1459. Unlike other barns in the area, the example at Landbeach is quite compact, with a delicate thatched roof and squat, square doors, making it unique in Cambridgeshire.

Landbeach Tithe Barn. Rethatching in progress. (Tithe Barn Trust/www.tithebarntrust.org.uk)

It was once under ownership of the Diocese of Ely, but was eventually purchased by South Cambridgeshire District Council in 1986.

Ely itself had a monumental stone barn called the Sextry Barn. Its title referred to the sacristan who was said to be responsible for various contents within the church. Its appearance was similar to those found much further west in Gloucestershire and Somerset, with plentiful buttresses and imposing gable ends which were exposed sometime in its history as ruins near to Ely Cathedral. Despite dating from as early as the thirteenth century and possibly being one of the largest in Europe, its demise came through demolition in 1842. This left Ely's other notable barn, the Monastic Barn, as the remaining such structure in the city. This barn, built some 300 years later in 1575 and also of stone, was the primary storehouse for the monastery but, unlike the Sextry Barn, may not have stored tithes. Today it forms part of Kings Ely's school offices.

Travelling in a wide arc around the edge of East Anglia's coast offers a rough route through the selection of towns and villages that host the area's remaining barns. In Norfolk's village of Dersingham, a barn built by the influential Pell family stands within the churchyard and though its position and title suggest that it was a tithe barn, no evidence has ever been offered to confirm this. Its listing as an ancient monument indicates two threshing barns built together, as well as the fact that it may have been heightened at some stage. This may explain the patchy but refreshingly unusual brick dressings. An inscription on the gable end reads '1671 July 31', which was most likely the date of construction. Eventually it was bequeathed to the local council in 1972 by Queen Elizabeth II, whose home at Sandringham lies just a mile or so south of the village, and it now stores masonry and other materials used to maintain other notable Norfolk buildings.

Dersingham Tithe Barn, Norfolk. The single, central buttress tells of its construction as two separate threshing barns. (Author)

The theme of red brick cladding continues further east at Horstead, north of Norwich, though perhaps in a way that detracts from the appearance of the village's barn. Dating from the same century as Dersingham's, this particular tithe barn is instead used today as the village community hub. This is apparent from the outside, looking similar to village halls built much more recently. Inside, old wooden beams can still be noticed from the gallery, joined now by modern sports facilities, heating, insulation and a sound system. Its continued use is commendable, preferable to allowing it to decay entirely as a vacant store, but little of its agricultural heritage is evident in its current form. Wroxham Barns, a notable farm nearby hosting artisan retail lots, also makes use of brick-built barns, though none are ever thought to have been related to tithing.

The return to black wood panelling comes at Sisland, located inland from Great Yarmouth and Lowestoft, where a large barn stands at one end of the widely spread village. It forms a set of accommodation lots for holidaymakers and little is known of its history prior to being converted. This situation repeats itself with the barn at Wattisham, further south and into Suffolk.

Accommodation also dominates the theme for the tithe barn at Brome, also in Suffolk, near the town of Diss. Here, what has been referred to historically as the Capital Barn sits within the Best Western Hotel formed from the sixteenth-century coaching inn at Brome Grange. Oddly, despite some considerable history highlighted best in Fiona Rule's *The Story of Brome Grange*, none of the buildings appear listed, perhaps explaining why the barn is shrouded on all sides by lean-tos and extensions. Inside, these 'bolt-ons' are clearly denoted by differences in the wood, but at the centre where the original barn structure is, evidence of rigging holes similar to those in Bedford's tithe barn can be seen in larger pieces of timber.

In the heart of Suffolk, Stowmarket's Museum of East Anglian Life does much to shed light on the working life in the area, with the on-site barn depicting elements of Suffolk's agricultural history. In the thirteenth century, this barn was built to store tithes from the Stowmarket area made payable to St Osyth's Abbey in Essex. At the time it would have been one of the longest barns in the area, thatched and with basic wattle and daub walls surrounding the timber frame. Over centuries, alterations and repairs to the barn resulted in a variety of valuable building techniques being demonstrated within the structure and eventually, by the nineteenth century, the roof was tiled and the walls weatherboarded. The barn was part of the farm's productivity during the Second World War, assisted by the Land Army, and was used throughout its farming life for threshing. Part of its impressive length was lost during a storm in the spring of 1968, but subsequent restoration and inclusion as the current museum's centrepiece have seen the Grade II listed building preserved for future generations to appreciate.

Perhaps the most attractive example in Suffolk, though, is the tithe barn fronting the main road through Sproughton on the outskirts of Ipswich. Dating from the late sixteenth century, its condition had deteriorated somewhat by the mid-1970s and the local parish council elected to gently restore the barn so that it could be used by the community once again. What results is a commendable effort to keep the exterior of the barn as authentic as possible, most notably with a newly thatched roof and neat, black wooden cladding. From the roadside, this looks suitably impressive, as do the two large porches that exist within the courtyard on the other side of the building. Inside, facilities to keep the barn in regular use include a sports hall floor, toilets, a kitchen and an extension with small shed-like structures at either end – one of which houses the quaint village shop. The tithe barn therefore maintains its importance in the village setting, not something that can be said of other barns that have been converted for private use.

Upon entering Essex, Britain's status as an island nation begins to appear through the proximity to busy ports at Harwich and Felixstowe and the saturation of freight traffic on the roads heading in and out of London. Towns like Witham, with its large industrial estates off the A12, become unlikely places for historic farm buildings to exist but in the villages and hamlets around them, notable examples do remain.

Many are quick to recognise the council-owned Cressing Temple Barns between Witham and Braintree. Though the former manor distances itself from the notion of tithe barns (as none were used for this purpose despite their similarity), its three examples are arguably some of the most important buildings that Britain has to offer. The site's past goes back to the Knights Templar's receipt of the Manor at Cressing in 1136 and it is during their presence that the Barley and Wheat barns were erected between 1205 and 1230, and 1257 and 1280 respectively, making these the oldest such barns in the world. Funds raised by the estate, which was involved in milling, baking, brewing and smithing, were sent onwards to those on Crusades in the Middle East before being transferred to the Knights Hospitaller in 1312, who may have moved the Barley Barn from elsewhere on the site. When the order was dissolved by Henry VIII in 1540, the manor and its barns went through a succession of private owners who repaired, rebuilt and amended the structure of the barns over time.

The current museum is dedicated to the construction techniques and methods used over many centuries and this knowledge can be broadly applied to barns of all types and

Sproughton Tithe Barn. Still very much a relevant focal point for the village. (Author)

sizes across the UK, including tithe barns in Essex and Kent specifically. The style of these buildings was largely necessitated by the need to support the heavy roof (tiled or thatched) and allow for as vast a space as possible to exist underneath it. The use of geometric shapes in planning the layout of each barn, studied in detail by the late Adrian Gibson MBE, shows that despite the sometimes crude appearance of barns in their present guise, these structures were no less technical than the modern steel barns seen aiding farmers in today's agricultural industry.

The style expressed by the barns at Cressing Temple is loosely duplicated at nearby Coggeshall in a barn dating from 1240. Coggeshall Abbey, a Cistercian establishment, sought not only to store tithes but wished to build a structure of a size that would display their power to the local people. As a result it was built in a prominent position overlooking the rest of the village. Unfortunately, this wasn't a true reflection of the abbey at all, defined instead by feuds with the wider church authority and significant debt by the time of its dissolution and sale in 1538. By the 1980s the barn was no longer fit for purpose as an agricultural store and had seen much neglect in the preceding decades. Five years after restoration work began in 1984, it was donated to the National Trust who have maintained it to a standard close to that of the barns at Cressing.

As England's landmass stretches ever-closer to the European continent and its own wealth of tithe barns in France, Belgium and Germany, such buildings become a regular Kentish feature despite the noted loss of examples at places like Nettlestead and Davington. A comprehensive archaeological study of barns in Kent, together with architectural descriptions and diagrams, was made in 1967 by S. E. Rigold, who also pointed out the dubiousness with which the term 'tithe barn' is used. He also expanded

Coggeshall Tithe Barn. The barn's layout stems from work carried out in 1381, before being fully restored to its current appearance in the 1980s. (Author)

on the eastern trend of building barns from wood, rather than the large stone barns of western England.

Many of Kent's towns and villages maintain their ageing barns, often as facilities within celebrated medieval settings. Prominent examples at Knole House near Sevenoaks and Maidstone can be misleading as to their purpose. The former is now a fully modernised conservation studio for the National Trust, having seen major alterations to its roof over time, and never likely stored tithes. Its immaculate interior is graced with UV filters, temperature and humidity controls as well as numerous floors keeping some of the Trust's many treasures secure.

In Maidstone, the large barn would once have been part of the Archbishop's Palace complex and it was built around the same time as the church in the fourteenth century. It may have initially stored tithes, but soon after it became stables for the Archbishop of Canterbury. In 1913, it was reported that interest from an American buyer had potentially threatened the barn with export state-side but today it remains as host for the musty and authentic atmosphere of the Maidstone Carriage Museum and is separated from other Palace buildings by the busy A229.

The small village of Lenham, now also partly defined by a major A-road, offers up a barn much more in line with expectations. It sits behind the timber-framed façades of the village centre to the side of St Mary's Church, with black timber walls and a huge tiled roof. Another adjacent barn was burned down in 1962 and today the cottages surrounding the late fourteenth-century survivor offer hints of medieval origins, with fragments of old stone gently presenting themselves on one gable end. As with most of the local amenities, the tithe barn upholds authenticity of the old English village and is used now to host art

Maidstone Carriage Museum. (Thomas Rogers)

Chilham Village Hall. The main hall was once the tithe barn, before being extended and added to over subsequent centuries. (Author)

exhibitions, talks and seasonal markets for the benefit of residents and those detouring from their journey along the A20.

A similar use and setting is found at the equally attractive village of Chilham further east. Its tithe barn is also used as a focal point for locals, but in an official capacity as the village hall. The structure is one of many parts: a larger fifteenth-century portion once acted as the place to store produce for the nearby castle; a smaller section was added in the 1930s. Unlike other large tithe barns, its appearance is therefore not one of a long, seamless space but is instead more varied. Still, the timber framing and red brick on the walls add to the pristine nature of it and other buildings in the area. Another notable barn at nearby Bagham, once used by the farmhouse and not thought to be a tithe barn, now hosts a popular antiques dealer.

Most of the tithe barns in this area, including Lenham, came under the authority of St Augustine's Abbey in Canterbury. This was also the case for Littlebourne, located very close to the city, whose tithe barn was used continuously for agriculture until the 1960s. It remains one of the longest in the country and, though it is widely cited to have been built around 1340, it is possible that its construction utilised elements of a previous twelfth-century barn. Preservation of the barn became the focus after Canterbury Council purchased it and the adjoining land in 1991 and it now opens its doors to the public on selected heritage open days.

Upon journeying through Kent to find these highlighted examples, the eye is undoubtedly drawn to other barns advertised on major routes that have since become refined accommodation options at places such as Evenhill or the Winter Barns at Nackington, which date from 1660. As the narrative of this title has suggested throughout, storing of tithes is not something easily proven with the majority of these examples.

5

The South and the West Country

Venturing around London's periphery and onward to the bountiful supply of barns in the south-west first warrants a look at East Sussex and Surrey, with the latter having records alluding to the payment of flowers as tithes for use in decoration during religious ceremonies in addition to the expected variety of crops. Falmer and Alciston provide two examples on the East Sussex coast, some distance from their neighbours in Surrey.

Shrouded almost entirely by extensions and additions is the venue space formed by the ancillaries at the Burford Bridge Hotel, near Box Hill and Dorking. The current coaching inn, altered significantly on the site of previous watering holes and hotels, saw guests passing through the area at the dawn of the motorcar age and grew over decades to a concern defined by its proximity to the M25, London and Gatwick Airport. In the mid-1930s, further work was carried out, including the positioning of a seventeenth-century tithe barn within its grounds, which was moved from Abinger Manor some five miles away. Alterations at this time were overseen by Baron Farrer of Abinger, whose interest in the hotel tied in with his position within the National Trust and their acquisition of land at Box Hill in the 1920s.

The moving of a barn also occurred at Loseley Park further west near Guildford, long-time residence of the More-Molyneux family. Built from the ruins of Waverley Abbey, England's oldest Cistercian Abbey, it is not surprising that the estate was entitled to some tithes or rent charges in the 1600s. In 1644 Sir Poynings More, then a Member of Parliament for Haslemere, sought to increase his tithes, perhaps to pay off debt. It is therefore not unreasonable to assume that the barn, built around 1633, may have been used to store tithes, or certainly produce farmed from the lands around the house. However, the barn was moved to its current position in 1982 by the late Fred Gooch and was amalgamated with another barn, as detailed in a Loseley Park brochure from 1988. It is unknown whether this movement was from elsewhere on the estate or from a nearby village or manor (as with the example at Box Hill) or where the involvement of a second barn originates.

Both barns have since become commercial ventures, with Mercure occupying the Burford Bridge Hotel and offering the barn as both a wedding venue and conference facility for those conducting business in and around an ever-active part of Britain. Similarly at Loseley Park, weddings and other special events now see the barn used throughout the year. Another notable barn, suggested to be a tithe barn by locals, also exists on the edge of the park in the hamlet of Littleton and is currently being converted to office space.

Perhaps the area's most notable barn is that at Wanborough, though this is adamantly and correctly advertised as a grange barn and not a tithe barn. It was built in 1388 and housed crops for Waverley Abbey until its demise. Its use continued, however, throughout the centuries and in 1705 the barn was extended, indicating growth in the associated farm's yield. It is surrounded by other barns and outbuildings, some of considerable age, and by the Church of St Bartholomew that was first built in 1060. Other old barns exist at Puttenham further south, a village distinguished by its brick walls around the priory though again none seem to have any connection to tithing. One is now used as an 'eco camping barn'.

Hampshire, too, contains examples unlikely to have stored tithes but which, nevertheless, add to the varying styles and history of large, medieval farm buildings. Of significance is the Great Barn at Old Basing situated between the current railway line and derelict canal near Basingstoke. The substantial brick barn was built in 1534 by 1st Marquess of Winchester to house vast yields in preparation for visits by Henry VIII, who favoured Basing House's hunting grounds above many others in the country. Hosting the King was quite an occasion, warranting the stockpiling of produce for feasting and entertainment which, in subsequent years, led to funds being diverted from the monumental house, which now lies in ruin across the road from the grange and the present-day visitor centre.

This image from a 1921 book about Surrey is thought to depict the grange barn at Wanborough. (Author's collection)

The barn itself did not go unscathed throughout history, however, playing a crucial part in the siege of Basing House during the English Civil War. Then under the Royalist 5th Marquess of Winchester, John Paulet, the house was engaged multiple times during the mid-1640s. One such engagement saw Parliamentarians storm the grange and barn to find plentiful supplies of food and a substantial place to hold against retaliating Royalists. As a result, not wishing to hand the valuable produce to the enemy, the Royalists regrouped and began attacking the barn themselves with the Parliamentarians holed-up inside. The resulting damage from artillery can still be seen in the walls of the barn and its involvement in warfare gave it an alternative name: the Bloody Barn.

The house eventually succumbed to Cromwell and the Parliamentarians in October 1645 and was dismantled to form a ruined footprint of the once grand house. The barn remains as a prime example of the effort made to support a Tudor manor and contemporary findings have cemented its importance as an Ancient Monument. Dendrochronology even suggests that the source of its timber was also used to build the famous *Mary Rose* in 1510 (or possibly its rebuild in 1536) and its vast interior, while largely left vacant, has been utilised to dramatic effect in films such as 2016's *Pride and Prejudice and Zombies*.

Barns elsewhere in Hampshire have slightly less obvious origins and the example near Petersfield offers up little information about its past. What is known is that it was likely

In addition to the 'Bloody Barn' at Basing House, another old barn (pictured) fronts The Street running through the village. (Author)

a barn allied to Durford Abbey after the land at Ditcham was given to it in 1273. The site of the former abbey (sometimes spelt Dureford) sits just over the border in West Sussex. The tithe barn's present form features unusually prominent vaulted stonework inside and its clean appearance is one of both masonry and carpentry altered and restored from the original structure during the nineteenth and twentieth centuries.

Ropley, a village just to the west of Petersfield, today is somewhat scarred by the fire-damaged Church of St Peter that sits at its centre, though work has now commenced to return it to glory. Nearby, a modernised private dwelling occupies the Parsonage Tithe Barn, which may have at one time collected tithes paid to the Augustinian Merton Priory – demolished in 1538 and now replaced by a Sainsbury's in the London Borough of Merton.

A pocket of picturesque farms and villages, nestled in the 'V' shape formed by the A34 and M3 between Andover and Winchester, yields two more barns, neither with an evidential tithe-storing purpose. The largest is the part-tiled, part-thatched barn at Borough Farm near Micheldever (which dates from the seventeenth century), while the one within the grounds of the luxurious Norton Park Hotel (and similarly dated) is styled more like examples in Kent and Essex.

Towards the coast, influence from two sizeable abbeys in Titchfield and Beaulieu dictate the history of the barns connected to them. At Titchfield, the fifteenth-century barn dominates the land around it with considerable length and mottled grey stonework. Originally, its appearance may have been more like the above example at Norton with weatherboarding on all sides, but an abundance of stonework through alterations within the abbey saw much of this replaced, over a century after it was originally constructed. Beaulieu, in addition to its outlying granges further afield, required the storage of produce from its own land and this is seen most impressively at St Leonard's Grange where the ruins of the medieval barn can be seen next to a more recent sixteenth-century example.

Borough Farm near Micheldever. Despite being unique in appearance, not much is known about the barn's past. (Author)

44

Across the Solent, the Isle of Wight, too, hosts a small number of buildings to hold the title of tithe barn, most with a new-found purpose in providing accommodation for tourists. On the east of the island, the Priory Bay Hotel has one among its outbuildings and another exists at Little Upton Farm. Interestingly at Freshwater, nearer to the famous Needles, the Parish Hall is housed within a former seventeenth-century tithe barn adjoined to the rectory chapel.

The county of Dorset has one of the larger concentrations of medieval barns in England, many of which are referred to as tithe barns. This warranted the publication of Jo Draper's thoroughly illustrated book *Dorset Barns* in 2010, with photography courtesy of David Bailey CBE.

Beginning within the Winterbornes, a collection of villages and hamlets surrounding Dorchester and Blandford Forum all prefixed with 'Winterborne' or 'Winterbourne', the rolling hills and patches of woodland denote a landscape different from that of the Jurassic Coast or Purbeck. Winterborne Clenston, nestled in a valley between Winterbornes Stickland and Whitechurch, hosts a sixteenth-century manor barn with a distinctive and rare chequered roof tile pattern. The rouge and noir tint to the alternating tiles makes for an attractive landmark and is thought to be the result of tiles being lifted from an older structure, possibly at nearby Milton Abbey. Material from the abbey's own tithe barn was reportedly used in building Capability Brown's landscaped village Milton Abbas in the 1770s.

Winterborne Clenston Manor Barn. (Author)

Sadly, the importance and appeal of the barn's exterior is tarnished by severe neglect in recent decades and, with a significant part of the roof patched by English Heritage in 2008, the building nears a very real risk of collapse. Conflicting agendas rooted in village politics reportedly see locals crucially linked to its survival playing a hard game with larger trusts and organisations in order to raise funds for repair, with each day of stalemate seeing further damage to the ageing barn. As much as £3 million is supposedly required to begin restoring the barn to a usable standard.

Further east, another collection of hamlets, the Tarrants, also contain a tithe barn within the ruins of Tarrant Abbey, at Tarrant Crawford. Such is the number of outbuildings within the area, it can be hard to pinpoint exactly which was the barn used to store tithes, if any at all. The neglected barn to the north-east, sometimes mistaken as the tithe barn, is seen partially roofless despite being rebuilt in 1759, whereas the actual tithe barn sitting perpendicular remains intact following alterations over the last 200 years. Both barns have origins in the fifteenth century.

Iwerne Courtney, north of Blandford, has something of a split personality with the locals' insistence on it being called Shroton so strong as to warrant both names being included on road signs. This oddity of rural place names initially poses a small hurdle in finding facts on the local barn and its mention in this title is largely down to a chance conversation with a Dorset native.

The barn is found within a range of outbuildings north of the church and presents an unusual U-shape when viewed from above. The two wings protrude outwards from the

Iwerne Courtney (or Shroton) Tithe Barn. (Author)

main nine-bay area, topped by a finely kept thatched roof. It may have been built in the 1600s when the church was rebuilt, but it likely originated sometime later in 1700s. Inside, eighteenth-century graffiti can been seen carved into the local stone and it is believed by some locals that this may have been a way to denote what crops were stored inside and by whom, though this has not been proven. The concept of produce belonging to a variety of farmers points to the barn being somewhat communal, possibly in connection with Cerne Abbey, who presided over another barn nearby at Hinton St Mary.

The extent of land overseen by Cerne Abbey prior to its demise in 1539 is obvious from its reported links to other Dorset barns and, looking at the facilities within the remains of the abbey and surrounding village, it is clear it had a great need to store agricultural produce. Records show that Cerne Abbey had a much larger income than that of Milton, Abbotsbury and Sherborne Abbeys in 1086 and 1291. Frustratingly, the fundamental confusion afflicting so many barns in this title is seen so clearly in the present village of Cerne Abbas, where two ageing barns still exist as part of the former abbey complex.

The barn to the north of where the abbey once stood, near the world-renowned Cerne Abbas Giant, is depicted by the Cerne Historical Society as a tithe barn and certainly its age, appearance and proximity to the abbey might suggest that this was the case. The CHS describe this barn as being used for the 'daily needs of the abbey' and, if this meant storing produce farmed from the immediate land around it, might instead signify that this barn was an abbey barn. Away from the abbey, at Barton Farm, is the much more ornate fourteenth-century barn more commonly referred to as the tithe barn. Arched windows and a small chimney in its southern half are the result of a thorough eighteenth-century conversion into a private dwelling, while the remaining bays maintain original features. Oddly, this barn is referred to as 'the main Abbey Barn', further complicating its use with that of the northern example and implying that perhaps both barns were used at one time to interchangeably store produce from both the abbey itself and from tithes earned from elsewhere. Both examples now see use as private dwellings and are intertwined with the attractive and far-reaching history of one of Dorset's most popular villages.

A similar situation affects the large, impressive complex of buildings at Whitcombe Manor, near Dorchester. The small barn facing Whitcombe Church is apocryphally named the tithe barn in local magazines and websites, but in fact the larger barn to its south-east displays many more bays and two porches, which form the kind of layout needed to store produce (either as tithes or for the manor). However, it is possible neither had any involvement with the church whatsoever, being built in the seventeenth and eighteenth centuries respectively, after ownership was passed over from the church, and while the latter has the architectural hallmarks of a typical former tithe barn, its current use is primarily for the rearing and delivering of lambs in the spring.

A much more obvious church connection exists at the barn in the secluded village of Symondsbury further west, whose tangible history comes in the form of a selection of fifteenth-century buildings. One of these, nestled at the heart of the long-standing Symondsbury Estate, is a large barn thought to have been constructed in *c.* 1440 and is possibly the third largest in Dorset.

As with other barns, initially it held much of the parish's hay and grain and was recorded as another abbey barn for Cerne Abbey. Only later was the term tithe barn used and, following the dissolution of the monasteries, Symondsbury Manor, the adjoining land and

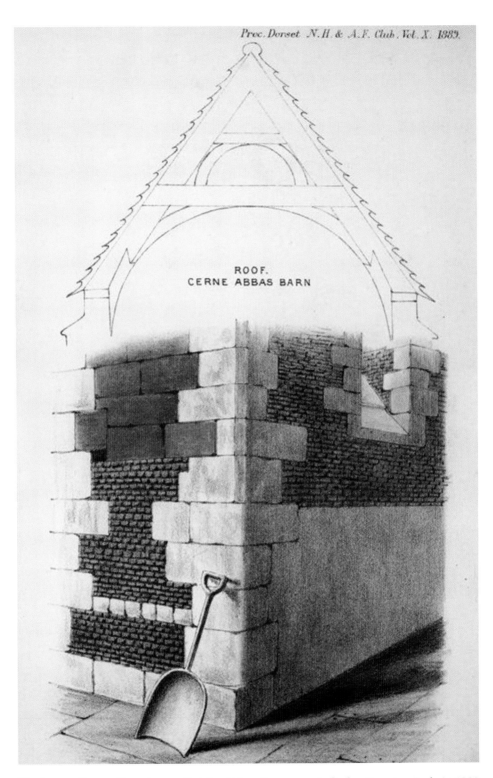

Proc. Dorset N.H. & A.F. Club. Vol. X. 1889.

ROOF.
CERNE ABBAS BARN

The barn at Barton Farm, here called the Abbey Barn, was studied quite extensively in 1889 by the Dorset Natural History and Archaeological Society. (Author's collection)

associated tithes changed hands between numerous dukes and earls. By the late 1880s, the estate came under ownership of the local Colfox family, whose origins began as farmers in the village, before becoming more prominent in nearby Bridport.

Under private ownership, the barn likely kept true to its purpose as an agricultural store, but saw wider use as industry changed in the 1900s. The thatched roof was replaced by tile in the 1930s along with some structural elements and, by then, the focus of farming in the area was more pastoral. The outbreak of the Second World War in 1939 saw the Home Guard utilise the barn's length for a rifle range and armoury, ominously looked over by the now distinctive Scots Pine trees on Colmer's Hill that were reportedly planted following the end of the First World War.

The Colfox family subsequently grew the estate as the village's primary business concern and began to renovate the plentiful outbuildings around the manor for a wide variety of uses. Today, surrounded by a cafe, cycle shop, art studio and holiday lets, the tithe barn now hosts numerous local events, music concerts, balls and weddings, expanding its appeal to the wider area as well as the local community. A thorough and largely considerate overhaul in 2014 invested roof lights and underfloor heating as well as fitting a wooden mezzanine, toilets and bar facilities.

Famed local author Thomas Hardy, whose tales take place within his altered iteration of the county, had his novel *Far From the Madding Crowd* hit the big screen in 2015 and during the film's production the tithe barn at Symondsbury was used to store props and equipment.

Despite this, notable period features still exist and barely legible carvings within the lias stone can still be seen beneath a more recent coat of paint. While the woodwork in the roof has been renewed, aged beams still lie embedded in the walls whose cream and golden tinge belies continuity with other estates near the Dorset/Somerset border.

Symondsbury Tithe Barn. Flax for Bridport's rope-making industry may also have been stored here, though from 1696 it was not subject to tithing. (Author, with kind permission of the Symondsbury Estate)

The adjoined barns at Wyke Farm, near Sherborne. (Author)

Sitting close to this border are the tithe barns at Wyke Farm, just east from the village of Bradford Abbas. Passengers travelling by rail between Yeovil Junction and Sherborne will have no doubt seen the distinctively long structures (of twelve and seven bays respectively) and could be forgiven for assuming the building to be one barn. As previously within its jurisdiction, it is possible that grain stored at Wyke was offered in support of Sherborne Abbey, however the buildings date from the sixteenth century, during which time the abbey was surrendered to Henry VIII and instead became the town's parish church. Curiously, the barns were chosen as one of approximately 1,500 subjects painted for the Second World War's Recording Britain project, which saw notable artists depict a variety of towns, villages and landscapes with the aim of capturing national pride. Thomas Hennell, who served as an official wartime artist, painted the barns from the direction of the railway line and shows clearly the many stone buttresses lining the walls – a far cry from V-1 launch sites he went on to paint in the battlefield. After seeing conflict in Belgium, Holland, India, Burma and Singapore, Hennell was captured and presumed killed in Java in 1945. His painting of the barns at Wyke is stored at the V&A in London.

Another major presence in the county was the Abbey of St Peter in Abbotsbury. Its barn was built in 1390 (some 300 years after the founding of the abbey in 1040) and has claims to once being the longest in Europe, part of the largest re-thatching in the UK, and still claims

Cotley Tithe Barn, near Chard. Another barn close to the borders of Devon, Somerset and Dorset. (Author, with kind permission of Tom Eames)

to be the longest thatched barn in Britain, despite part of it now being ruined. Tithes were collected from some twenty-two villages located on land owned by the abbey, warranting a structure of its height and length to accommodate vast amounts of grain. Remains of small, prehistoric fossils can be seen in some areas of its construction highlighting its position on the Jurassic Coast between Lyme Regis and Portland.

The barn's survival likely resulted from wealth, in the form of land and its tithes, being inherited by Henry VIII after he, through Giles Strangways, destroyed the abbey in 1539. Subsequently Strangways purchased Abbotsbury for a sum of £1,096 from the King and his name still resides in the owners of Ilchester Estates, who own the abbey grounds today. The barn and land around it now sees use as a family attraction, incorporating a small farmyard zoo and indoor play area, making the term 'play barn' perhaps more accurate here than at other such facilities elsewhere in the country. It is also clearly a popular landmark in Dorset and has featured heavily on postcards and in guidebooks even when in competition with other abbeys and barns in the county.

Southward towards the ever-narrowing landmass of Cornwall, the concentration of publicly accessible tithe barns similarly decreases. Many of the large farms and rural estates in the county of Devon have converted barns, since enclosed by electric gates and CCTV-covered pastures. As a result, researching their history and determining their legitimacy can be difficult and while notably converted examples exist in places such as Huxham, near Exeter and Ashburton, their smart, clean and largely tasteful

Abbotsbury Tithe Barn, Dorset. (Author's collection)

transformations into holiday cottages and outbuildings make them somewhat worthless to those taking an interest in their former use. Others are notoriously difficult to locate such as the example at Broadhembury's Grange in East Devon, despite having been used during the Second World War 'in connection with camouflage work' and being tied to Dunkeswell Abbey. The form of tithes in Devon likely varied, encompassing crops, livestock and fish: Sheila Bird's 1986 *Companion to Seaton, Beer & Branscombe* suggests that turbot, sole and plaice were reluctantly offered to 'men of cloth' as tithes in the past. In Lynmouth on the north coast, the disappearance of Irish herring from nearby waters after 1797 was blamed on the Church for demanding tithes from fishermen.

Thankfully, the lack of publicly accessible barns is more than outweighed by the significance of the county's two prominent examples, which exist alongside the great abbeys of Buckland and Torre. Both have tangible links to Sir Francis Drake, who is celebrated widely across the county, with Buckland Abbey being his home for some fifteen years. The barn here was used to store the produce of the Cistercian Abbey established in 1278 and at over 80 metres long and 8 metres high, is far more impressive than the now altered abbey building at its side. Dartmoor granite from Roborough Down was used to construct the barn, resulting in an appearance every bit as heavy as the material used to build it. Today it is used on occasion for events hosted by the abbey's present owners, the National Trust, otherwise lying vacant for those visiting to admire in its vast emptiness.

The example on the English Riviera also sees tourists gaze upon its timber and stone as part of a heritage attraction. Torre Abbey, in Torquay, refers to its tithe barn as the Spanish Barn owing to its use holding prisoners of war from the Spanish Armada during 1588.

Broadhembury Grange. The fourteenth-century barn is located behind the main house. (Author's collection)

Torre Abbey. The Spanish Barn is to the left, facing the coast. (Author's Collection)

Its size would have allowed some breathing space for the 397 sailors captured from the *Nuestra Senora del Rosario*, as it did for the grain and hay paid to the abbey over time. This barn is also allegedly Devon's oldest, with parts dating from the thirteenth and fifteenth centuries now among subsequent repairs made to the roof.

At the border with Cornwall, a small collection of cottages described as barns exist at Mead, near Welcombe. This isolated settlement, accessible off the A39 via a series of endlessly narrow and bleak lanes, seems to lie completely off the radar with few listed structures, landmarks or points of interest. However, Mead Farm is thought to have a history going back to the English Civil War. Until the 1950s, the building known as the 'Great Tythe Barn' was part of a working farm, housing cattle and crops on two floors, and remains one of only a few references to tithe barns in this area of England.

Another lies just north of Bude and within Cornwall's boundaries at Maer. It is estimated to have originated from the fourteenth century but over time it has been chopped and changed to keep up with the demands of agriculture, before being transformed into a stunning luxury home by local architects The Bazeley Partnership in 2015. Thankfully, some of the aged wood survives among polished glass and contemporary furniture and though the length of the barn once lay split, with one half bulked out with horrendous breeze blocks, this forms the basis for a transparent separation in the roof and the grey blocks are now covered by tasteful wooden cladding.

The barn at Maer is described by Cornish authorities, in a comprehensive breakdown of the region's agricultural buildings, as being the only 'known probable example' of a tithe barn left in the county and though other contenders exist at St Newlyn East, even further into Cornwall, their certainty is questioned on account of the existence of more recent, multi-storied chall barns.

The Tithe Barn, Maer, prior to restoration. (The Bazeley Partnership, Bude, Cornwall)

The Tithe Barn, Maer. The completed project was celebrated in the More 4 programme *Homes By the Sea*. (The Bazeley Partnership, Bude, Cornwall)

6

Somerset and Bristol

In contrast to Devon and Cornwall, the ceremonial county of Somerset is rife with medieval barns and abbeys and the glorious settings within which these ancient structures reside inspired the writing of this title. Such was the ecclesiastical strength of Somerset's famed landmarks in Glastonbury, Wells and Bath that their historic influence over towns and villages can be felt even at the county's extremities and in some cases beyond.

West Somerset, despite being a somewhat secluded arm of the county, hosts a selection of picturesque villages all within short distance of either Exmoor's national park boundary or the Quantock hills further east. Of those that contain tithe barns, the furthest inland is Fitzhead, which has a rather quaint and petite example thought to date from the fourteenth century. Regular efforts by a community tapping into the wider area's admirable trend for volunteering have resulted in another practical and usable venue for hosting local concerns. Unusual features, such as the select buttresses at the eastern end, braced chimney and glazed windows show its evolution away from a usable barn, most notably with the lack of any present doors big enough to accommodate carts. The barn's future resides with a local management committee who lease it from the Diocese of Bath and Wells.

Three more barns exist in this area along the route of the once proposed railway line from Taunton to Porlock, which only ever made it as far as the seaside town of Minehead in 1874, having previously terminated at Watchet. Had it reached the fringes of *Lorna Doone* territory, it would have passed by the village of Selworthy which, among its biscuit tin National Trust cottages, contains a tithe barn now used to provide bed and breakfast. The route, now hosting England's longest heritage railway, does however still pass through Stogumber nearer to Taunton and this village is recorded as having a thatched tithe barn around 1650, perhaps referring to the current barn situated behind St Mary's Church. Its interior provided villagers with an apt coal store during the twentieth century and now its exterior provides passers-by with a prime example of walls resembling the red sandstone from Triscombe Quarry located nearby. Ivy shrouded much of the building in the early 1980s but following a clean-up in 1998 by English Heritage, it falls in line with the rest of the local setting, which nears perfection when it comes to the authenticity of a typical English village.

Equally as authentic, if not substantially more commercialised, is Dunster village, also passed by steam trains nearing the end of their journey at Minehead. Here stands the impressive legacy left by the Luttrell family, including Dunster Castle. At one time, it and the surrounding land was owned by the Crown Estate and this included the village tithe barn, located behind

Right: Fitzhead Tithe Barn.
(Author)

Below: The Tithe Barn,
Selworthy. What might have
been a 'dole window' can
be seen on the wall facing
the road. It may also have
been used to deposit tithes.
(Author)

Church Street. Unlike many examples in this title, Dunster's tithe barn was indisputably used to collect tithes for the adjacent priory and in 1535, shortly before its dissolution, was recorded as passing on £6 13s 7d of income to its superiors in Bath. Records of tithes passing through Dunster can be found as far back as the eleventh century and this extensive past also suggests that the current building, thought to be sixteenth century, was built upon the foundations of previous barns. A plan of the area from 1735 clearly shows three rooms built into the thick walls of the current barn, marking them as straw houses, and these interesting features remain today as utility rooms for the barn's event hosting and wedding receptions.

The barn's current appearance, restored to a very high standard, resulted from many elements of a project by the Dunster Tithe Barn Community Hall Trust, who sought assistance from the Somerset Buildings Preservation Trust, the Crown Estate and local authorities to secure and use the £555,000 needed to tastefully and considerately form an appropriate amenity for the village. The interior, now a bright white, still retains the countless daisy wheels etched into the walls, corner rooms and aged timbers (carbon dated to 1614) but is enhanced by its mezzanine floor, underfloor heating and modified acoustics, as well as an attached reception building and spacious courtyard. Its well-kept historical features, well-documented place in Dunster's past, and the affection in which it is held by those involved with it are no doubt responsible for its capacity to intrigue tourists and please locals in equal measure: a common theme in this part of Somerset.

Above and opposite: : Dunster Tithe Barn. One of many notable landmarks in the historic village. (Author, with kind permission of Dunster Tithe Barn)

Elsewhere in the county, the territorial claims by each of the different abbeys can be still be loosely determined by the remaining tithe barns which provided them with income. At West Camel, north of glove-making town Yeovil, the large barn sitting mostly out of view behind the Old Rectory is unusual in not obviously displaying the gorgeous orange Hamstone used to construct many buildings in this part of Somerset. Thought to date from the fifteenth century, the barn would have been part of a grange, storing produce for Muchelney Abbey until its dissolution, much like another nearby example at Somerton. This former barn, sat to the east of the town next to the Parsonage, was transferred after the dissolution to Bristol Cathedral along with the local tithes. Today the building, whose predecessor was severely damaged in 1759 and rebuilt over subsequent years, is split into three private properties, the centre house making use of the tall cart entrance.

Somerton's tithe barn does show the characteristically attractive burnt orange tinge of the locally sourced Hamstone, but not quite as impressively as Stoke-sub-Hamdon Priory at the base of Ham Hill, from where the stone is quarried. Here, a partially thatched threshing barn with fifteenth-century origins sits at the centre of the priory now owned by the National Trust, who propose that it was once used to store tithes in support of the medieval college community that existed on site.

Hamstone also dresses what is commonly referred to as Somerset's largest barn at Preston Plucknett, now a busy suburb of Yeovil. It and the surrounding farm buildings, now part of Yeovil Business Centre, erroneously take on the term 'abbey' to describe both the farm and the barn despite there being little evidence to suggest that the site was ever ecclesiastical. In 1951 it was even listed as a tithe barn by Historic England and much of the confusion may have stemmed from a transfer of ownership to Lady Georgiana Fane in 1841. The barn was likely built some 400 years earlier by John Stourton to accommodate wool and was originally thatched. Some damage was dealt to the barn in 1940 as a result of German bombing and the thatch was lost entirely in the 1970s to fire. Today the barn is a showroom and storage facility for contractors and has been surrounded over the decades by housing necessitated by Yeovil's expanding population.

Perhaps the most obvious collection of medieval barns in Somerset are those built by Glastonbury Abbey in the villages surrounding a town now rife with spiritual connections and mystical qualities. The 1991 essay 'The Somerset Barns of Glastonbury Abbey' by C.J. Bond and J.B. Weller attempts to delve into the exact relationship that these remaining barns had with the abbey and (as with many of the reference works mentioned in this title) stumble across the common ambiguities over tithes, granges and how produce stored in these barns was actually used to benefit the abbey. Interestingly, Bond and Weller introduce the article by explaining the abbey's far-reaching influence and ownership of land in Dorset, Gloucestershire, Devon, Hampshire, Wiltshire and beyond (as well as approximately one-eighth of Somerset itself). In around 1275 a list of barns owned by Glastonbury that were damaged in a great storm included the villages of Marksbury, Walton, Wrington and Zoy alongside those villages where barns survived.

Of the four Glastonbury Abbey barns that are left, the one between West Pennard and West Bradley is the one most likely to have stored tithes in its past. Though the barn's parish allegiance is confused somewhat by its position on the present boundary between the two villages, the area's ties to Glastonbury are recorded numerous times in the thirteenth century, including the payment of tithes in 1291. Now owned by the National

West Pennard Court Barn. (Author)

Trust, the fifteenth-century barn looks squat compared to its remaining contemporaries, possibly due to its location at the centre of a large field and lack of a pitched roof above both central porches. Instead, an extended tile roof covers each doorway.

Dressings on this barn are of Doulting stone, a building material quarried since Roman times and noted for its creamy grey colour and apparent ability to sparkle in sunlight. Like the Hamstone of south Somerset, Doulting stone defines much of the Mendip area's settlements and can be seen implemented at Wells Cathedral and Glastonbury Abbey themselves. Within the village of Doulting, an eight-bay barn once under the Glastonbury umbrella exists at Manor Farm, this time with a double-porch format, but quite obviously built using the same stone found on its figurative doorstep. Its origins again are from the fifteenth century, well after the area was taken over by the abbey. The rise of more recent buildings around it, including the manor, have done nothing to remove its purpose as an agricultural store. Viewing the barn today, bails can be seen piled high around it, perhaps indicating its redundant size for the modern farmer, and two large yards face the porches on both north and south sides.

The largest of Glastonbury's remaining barns (some 33 metres long) at Pilton is also the one with arguably the most fascinating modern history and is the barn that sparked this author's interest in the subject of tithe barns following a chance encounter some years ago. Regrettably, its status as a former tithe barn, like others, comes under some dispute. However, in contrast with other barns, this is borne from a conflict of sources and not a lack of, or uncertain, evidence.

Previous barns would have existed on the site, at Cumhill Farm to the south of the village, and like those above, the importance of the parish to the abbey is well

Doulting Manor Barn. Still very much used as part of a working farm. (Author)

documented in the 1200s and earlier in the *Domesday Book* of 1086. An accompanying guide to the barn, published in 2008 by the Pilton Barn Trust, proposes that the barn would have stored produce farmed directly for the abbey and thus is an abbey barn, rather than a tithe barn. This is backed up by a further suggestion that another barn once stood within the grounds of St John's Church with the purpose of storing parish tithes, though a time frame for the existence of this barn is hard to determine. Despite this, the barn at Cumhill has been known throughout recent history as Pilton Tithe Barn, possibly as a result of the Ordnance Survey marking it as such on widely circulated maps throughout the twentieth century.

Aside from the singular, central porch, its appearance and size is very similar to the one at Doulting, to the extent that it has been suggested that the same masons and carpenters worked on both during the late fourteenth or early fifteenth century. Indeed, some of the stonework is of a notably high quality and at the top of each of the four gables are carvings representing the four Evangelists. For a time, it was only the hollow stone structure that was visible to Pilton's visitors following a devastating fire on 22 June 1963, the result of a lightning strike. Vivid accounts from firemen from as far as Taunton and Yeovil recall trying to prevent the stone from exploding, due to the fierce heat emanating from the many old oak timbers. Locals remember seeing the smoke from the surrounding towns and villages. A young Michael Eavis, of Glastonbury Festival fame, was known to have run in during the fire's infancy to save a tractor from inside. Indeed, tractors had been a common feature in the barn during the 1940s as they were used to train members of the Women's Land Army.

By the September of 1963, shortly after the fire, yet more dispute of its tithing use appeared in the *Cheddar Valley Gazette*, which sourced information from a former vicar broadcasting his views in an old issue of the *Shepton Mallet Illustrated Magazine*. Interestingly, the vicar conceded that the barn may have stored tithes at some stage during its extensive history but doubts that this was its original purpose.

The loss of the barn's roof prompted a great deal of interest over subsequent decades in restoring it to its former glory and, following the purchase of the barn by Michael Eavis in 1995, a brochure outlining the plans to apply for Heritage Lottery Funding and explaining its history to visitors was produced. Eventually, £400,000 was received, aided by a grant from English Heritage, and £240,000 came directly from the Glastonbury Festival, allowing work to commence on rebuilding the roof to a standard and style matching that of the original. Peter McCurdy, whose expertise in carpentry helped build the current Globe Theatre in London, secured the contract for the work, which was completed in 2005 and won numerous awards including the Best Use of British Timber at the same year's Worshipful Company of Carpenters Wood Awards. Eavis (later awarded a CBE for his charitable work) cites the work on the barn as something he is 'most proud of' during his active life in Pilton.

In many ways the barn at Pilton represents the typical life cycle of a medieval barn, having gone through Abbey ownership, post-dissolution agricultural purpose, use during war, devastating ruin and contemporary appreciation and restoration. It today remains one of the best examples of a hidden British landmark with a past to rival that of the nation's more renowned ones.

Above and left: Pilton's barn exemplifies the typical life of a tithe barn and ambiguity over the term. It is more likely to have been built as an abbey barn. (Author, with kind permission of the Pilton Barn Trust)

This in many ways makes Glastonbury's resident barn seem the weakest candidate of the four, again most likely an abbey barn storing its own produce and without the gripping narrative of Pilton's barn. However, it does have distinguishing features of its own and presents an apt introduction to medieval barns for visitors at Somerset's Rural Life Museum, of which it forms a part. It has a more specific decade of origin compared to the other three, being built in the 1340s, but does share some of their other features. Like Pilton, carvings depicting the four Evangelists exist on the exterior and, like Doulting, the quality of stonework suggests that the abbey was keen to project its wealth. Wheat and rye were the mainstays of the barn, stacked high at either side of the porches and threshing floor and, as with the other local barns, thought went into building a store that kept produce dark, aerated and vermin-free. Its location across the road from the abbey grounds shows how close a relationship the farmed land around it had with those working within it.

Following the dissolution of Glastonbury Abbey in 1539 and the hanging, drawing and quartering of the last Abbot at Glastonbury Tor, all of its barns were eventually passed into private hands (and for those that stored tithes so too did the right to receive them). In Glastonbury's case the barn became property of the Duke of Somerset, Edward Seymour. Farming remained on the site right through until 1974 when the Mapstone family donated it to the council to form the current museum. Shortly after the council received it, the barn saw fame as the setting for Barry Lyndon's duel with Lord Bullingdon in Stanley Kubrick's film *Barry Lyndon* of 1975. Kubrick reportedly came across the venue by chance via a location scout and sought to depict the occasion of a duel in a setting different from that offered by an exterior location (though he, like those reviewing the film afterwards, incorrectly referred to it as a tithe barn).

A somewhat spurious fifth barn related to those remaining from Glastonbury Abbey is worthy of a mention at Haselbury Mill near Crewkerne. While this area of Somerset might instead have encroached on the lands of Sherborne Abbey and includes a small tithe barn

Glastonbury Abbey Barn, now part of the Somerset Rural Life Museum. (Author)

at the centre of Merriott, the barn at Haselbury Mill actually bears no allegiance to any such church, abbey or monastery and never received produce of any kind, let alone tithes. Curiously, this barn was the result of mill owner Roger Bastable's desire to build what he refers to as the first 'tithe barn' in over 300 years.

As a friend of Michael Eavis, Bastable set about taking the design of the Pilton barn and recreating an approximation of it in Hamstone to form a venue for events, dinners, dances and weddings. Renowned stonemason Richard England, following a research visit to Pilton, headed a team of up to nine masons working seven days a week (except Christmas Day) and had the barn finished in 2008 with the wooden interior and roof formed from both English and French oak. A recycled finial from Wells Cathedral provided the sole period element to the structure, which was then opened by Eavis. Interestingly, lean-tos containing a kitchen and bar were needed due to the physical limitations on width for a building of that design, showing that others of a similar style, built many centuries prior, really were done so at their maximum possible dimensions.

The loss of its finial does little to detract from the domination of Wells Cathedral and the Bishop's Palace in the city, which also has a notable barn, known as the Bishop's Barn, on Silver Street. Like other buildings nearby, its walls were built from Doulting stone in around the fifteenth century and, through its proximity to the Bishop's Palace, it is thought to have stored tithes offered in the form of grain. Over time, the barn saw use during the Bloody Assizes, which were fallout from the Battle of Sedgemoor in 1685, to quarter

Haselbury Mill Tithe Barn was completed in 2008. (Author, with kind permission of Haselbury Mill)

Royalists but eventually became a much more positive venue hosting popular rock bands in the 1970s including Slade, Supertramp and Status Quo. These gigs were the brainchild of Gordon Poole, Tony Leach and Guy Bruer, who sought to utilise the barn for entertainment and, in typical Somerset style, employed facilities as basic as farm trailers to set the stage for some of the decade's biggest rock acts.

Further north, Somerset separates some of its ceremonial land to the present Bath and north-east Somerset area and, along with the Mendip region, has a landscape defined not by stretching acres of farmland, but by coal mining relics, dismantled railways and stone quarries which are still in use today. Unlike the Black Country, however, where the coal mining industry removed most of the agricultural land, this part of Somerset maintained its farming industry and, with it, some of its tithe barns.

Interestingly, the fourteenth-century barn in Mells isn't grouped with those mentioned previously, despite once coming under the jurisdiction of Glastonbury Abbey along with the rest of the village. Stylistically, it bears little resemblance to the others, with an offset porch on one side. In addition, having its interior modernised also separates it from the other Glastonbury barns, who are mostly vacant and untouched by such modifications.

At Midsomer Norton, the tithe barn's change of use is arguably unique. The squat but tall building now sits behind the busy high street but was once linked with Merton Priory

A promotional poster for Supertramp, who in 1970 had yet to release their biggest-selling album *Breakfast in America*. (www.gordonpoole.com)

near London as part of their outlying property. It was converted by the priory into a church sometime after its construction in the fifteenth century. Now known as the Church of the Holy Ghost, it has as much history as a place of worship as it likely has for the storing the village tithes. The characteristic porch on one side, opposed by a shorter doorway at the rear, cannot hide the building's original purpose, but the church windows and additional doorways, implemented by Giles Gilbert Scott, tell of its conversion – as does the gilt tabernacle inside, which is thought to have come from the Catholic chapel on Warwick Street in Westminster.

Other notable barns exist within the small and secluded villages toward Bath, such as those at Stanton Drew, home of the famous standing stones, and Norton Malreward, though both of these have since been converted into homes or holiday lets. Closer to the city, Saltford, too, has a former tithe barn converted for this use near the banks of the Avon and near an Anglo-Saxon burial ground. At Priston Mill, the age of its Tythe Barn (an unusual appearance of this spelling in the south-west) raises questions over its title, perhaps merely a commercial tag used in conjunction with its use as a wedding venue for both Bath and Bristol's couples.

But among these settlements is Englishcombe, a one-in-one-out village at the bottom of a valley just outside the suburban streets of Odd Down and Twerton. Here, a more recognisable tithe barn remains near the Church of St Peter – a notable fourteenth-century relic of Bath Abbey. It is now privately owned and has a bland but neat landscaped garden to frame the front of the barn and its porch, with the rear adjoining the rectory.

The continued use of Nailsea Tithe Barn, further west towards Weston-Super-Mare, is unique in the area, having seen a significant part of its life as a school, championed by renowned philanthropist Hannah More. Even before its opening for education in 1792, the barn was a key building in the town having been there since the late fifteenth century, possibly to store tithes for the rector at Wraxall, under whom Nailsea's Holy Trinity Church came. A rare period of vacancy in the late 1990s threatened the ageing barn with demolition, resulting in a campaign to save it from developers. The barn was reopened after a substantial but carefully considered modernisation and is now used for a variety of community events, once again playing a crucial part in Nailsea's society.

As with the larger cities in Britain's north, the unofficial capital of the West Country has slowly swallowed up a number of notable barns on its periphery. Towns and villages now part of Bristol's wider conurbation were once farming communities, many since losing their medieval barns. Indeed, the frequency of tithe barns in all of the surrounding counties and past influence of the former Augustinian Abbey indicate the strength of Bristol's religious power which saw tithe payments made from as far as Penarth, in Wales and Halberton in Devon.

Shirehampton, much closer to the city, is no doubt familiar to motorists as they pass over the Avonmouth Bridge. Among the tower blocks and motorway infrastructure is a ten-bay barn built in the late fifteenth century. While previously this area may have seen open views in the direction of the Bristol Channel, it is now surrounded by the suburban commercial properties on the high street, including a petrol station whose forecourt is shared with that of the barn. Unlikely links to the former Cormeilles Abbey in Normandy have been cited as the barn's purpose, which may well have been to store tithes, though today it instead provides space for a community venue in addition to one end of the barn forming an attractive cottage. The barn's current appearance is thought to be the result of changes in the seventeenth, nineteenth and twentieth centuries.

Like Shirehampton the settlements of Filton and Stoke Gifford (both in South Gloucestershire) have, in recent times, seen their borders mingle with those of Bristol's growing residential and commercial developments. Filton famously became the centre of aviation following the expansion of Filton Aerodrome and the appearance of companies involved in progressing Britain's aerospace technology during and after both World Wars. The existence of a tithe barn has been mentioned fleetingly in some accounts of the village, possibly associated with Filton House and while the evidence is lacking, Filton was one of the Gloucestershire villages from which Bristol Abbey received 'monastic payments' in the 1400s and 1500s. Interestingly, footage from 1949 of the maiden flight of the gargantuan Bristol Brabazon shows crowds assembled on a significantly dilapidated barn of considerable size, though linking this with references to the village tithe barn is pure speculation by this author.

At Stoke Gifford, it is the rail network that presides over what was once, like Filton, a community dominated by farming. Redevelopment of a site near to St Michael's Church

Right and overleaf: Nailsea Tithe Barn. In previous guises the original oak timbers and stone were clad with plasterboard shielding them from view. The restored barn displays these important features once again. (Author, with kind permission of Nailsea Town Council)

uncovered evidence of a structure thought to be a medieval barn and recent findings make reference to a tithe barn that remained until as recently as the 1980s. Had it remained, like the manorial barn at nearby Winterbourne, it would have seen crowds of people in and around Bristol Parkway railway station, heard the roar of Filton's innovate past and felt the endless flow of the M4's traffic.

7

The Cotswolds and London

Tracking old barns north of Bristol into Gloucestershire becomes an inevitable tour of the M5 motorway as it points traffic in the direction of Birmingham. At a number of junctions, small villages within earshot of the roar of tyres contain preserved examples very much in tune with the county's encroachment on the Cotswolds. The prevalence of high earners in this area makes the restoration, conversion or preservation of ageing, expensive buildings routine for those who are lucky enough to own or preside over them.

Junction 13 offers up the first notable barn, just south of Stonehouse in the village of Frocester where the commanding Estate Barn lies beyond the gatehouse of Frocester Court.

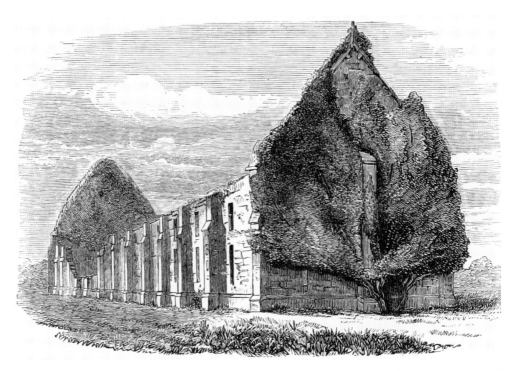

Sudeley Castle Tithe Barn. A rare example of a ruined barn in the Cotswolds. Many are restored for private endeavours. (Author's collection)

Its recorded history begins somewhere in the thirteenth century when Gloucester Abbey refers to John de Gamages' '*magna grangia*', or large barn, constructed between 1284 and 1306. The resulting structure remains one of the longest in England, with two porches facing in the direction of the court (built later in fifteenth century), which forms the basis for the surrounding estate. Interestingly, only one smaller doorway (denoting perhaps a one-way system) exists on the opposite side and another at one gable end. Elizabeth I visited the court in 1574 and the location of the village, between Gloucester and Bath, has been utilised over time by many, including the Romans. This wealth of history has seen Frocester featured in such high-profile settings as Channel 4's *Time Team*.

The barn's local limestone walls extend to approximately 68 metres adjacent to a small track sitting between Frocester Hill and Court Road south of Frocester's main settlement. The roof is a more recent feature, resulting from a significant fire somewhere in the barn's 700-year history. Oak beams are held together with tree nails and ironwork from the nineteenth century, topped with tiles made from Cotswold stone, which were restored over an eight-year period more recently by previous owner and late archaeologist Eddie Price. Despite restoration, the interior still resembles a look derived from techniques used throughout the medieval period to create a vast space for storage.

A mix of arable crops and livestock were kept sheltered by the barn as the estate changed and expanded its agriculture over time. Even today, its primary use is found in storing hay, tools and farming equipment, though present-day combine harvesters may differ somewhat from their medieval equivalents. The current setting of the barn is typical of Gloucestershire rural life and those curious enough to ask to look around the

An unidentified Gloucestershire barn, possibly near the course of the River Coln. (Author's collection)

barn are escorted through thick slurry and between cow sheds before passing through the enormous wooden doors to view inside.

Evidence that anything stored within the barn was used to pay tithes is scarce and the well-informed present-day owners attest its identity as an Estate Barn. Though its Grade I listing with Historic England refers to it as a tithe barn numerous times, it is possible that the storage of produce was a more personal endeavour by monks from St Peter's Abbey in Gloucester who owned the land at the time that it was built.

At Owlpen Manor, tucked in a secluded valley near Uley, a barn with significant alterations exists under the title 'Tithe Barn' with origins from the 1450s according to its oak A-frames. Certainly, in the twelfth century, the inhabitants of the manor, the de Olepenne family, were frequent contributors to St Peter's Abbey and offered up some of their own lands to them in 1174. That tithes in the form of produce were offered is not, therefore, a stretch of the imagination.

The rural A-roads on the border with Wiltshire and the Fosse Way reveal more notable tithe barns approaching Tetbury such as the one at Calcot Spa, built in the 1300s and once linked to Kingswood Abbey. Further along, the impressive Beverston Castle sits obscured out of view by a cloak of ancient trees and is surrounded by a number of outbuildings still used on the working farm. The most notable, the Pilgrims Barn, distances itself from the tithe barn format by having no door large enough for any type of relevant cart and instead its name derives from its likely use as accommodation at some stage in its 700-year history. During an uncertain time for the castle (up for sale at the time of writing) the barn houses maintenance equipment and a workshop.

Pilgrims Barn, Beverston, early 1900s. The roof of the tithe barn can be seen in the far background, just left of the Pilgrims Barn. (Author's Collection)

Behind this however lies another much larger barn, together with cow sheds and a dovecote, its form more closely resembling that of a tithe barn. It was built much later in the seventeenth century and features a cruciform layout with two opposing central porches, though one is now sealed. As part of Castle Farm, this barn actively fulfils its duties, storing large quantities of corn, though it is unlikely any is siphoned off to the church today. Interestingly, a very similar barn exists at Park Farm across the main road, also said to be a tithe barn and dating from the seventeenth century.

The Great Tythe Barn just outside of Tetbury does little to hide itself from view and is advertised with large signs from Newnton Road. Both it and the adjacent farmhouse show no signs of medieval history but still offer much in the way of a glimpse into the area's farming past. The house is thought to originate from around 1700 and though the Historic England listing for the barn suggests it was also built in the eighteenth century, the owner Julian Benton instead believes that the barn is the oldest building on the site and therefore pre-dates the house. In fact his knowledge and memories tell much about the life of the barn before its conversion to a venue some twenty-five years ago. Wheatsheafs were apparently stored to the full height of the barn ready for a travelling threshing machine (complete with staff and caravans) to come and process it and the barn also saw use as both a wool store and cart shed at some point in its past. Later it was used to store more modern machinery such as a tractors. Curiously, Benton also presents a tangible insight into the final days of the tithe system in Britain, during the late 1960s, when he received a letter from 'an office somewhere, I think in Kent' requesting that he formally pay off outstanding tithes owed by the farm prior to his ownership. 'It came to something like £8,' he recalls. The Great Tythe Barn also makes the claim of partly kickstarting the 'wedding barn' trend in the late 1990s and this is evidenced by the countless to-ing and fro-ing between himself and the local authorities to get the relevant permission for the mezzanine floors (possibly some of the largest to be implemented into a former tithe barn) and walkway connecting them. The two levels of ground flooring denote the barn's original construction in two phases, with the lower half being built first and the higher portion added some time later as an extension.

Returning to the M5 and travelling just a couple of junctions further north places motorists within spitting distance of another Gloucestershire barn at Brockworth, home of the famous cheese-rolling event at Cooper's Hill and the advancement in aeronautics of Frank Whittle's jet propulsion during the 1940s. On the outskirts of what it now a well-developed settlement lies Brockworth Court, an important medieval manor house once under the jurisdiction of Llanthony Secunda Priory before being handed to the Guise family by Henry VIII, who visited the property with Anne Boleyn in 1535.

The barn here is thought to have origins in the thirteenth century, though the history of the surrounding site goes back further to occupation by the Chandos family between 1121 and 1310. Its interior of eight bays was at one time extended, showing that the productivity of the site grew and possibly peaked during the late 1400s. Farming on the site continued well into the nineteenth and twentieth centuries before being finally scaled down in the 1960s. Following a fire in 1996, a mere shell of the barn existed, which comprised simply of the gable ends and buttresses, and an extensive overhaul took place shortly afterwards. Attractive timbers left inside, still with scorch marks, add to what is now a simple but inherently beautiful wedding venue that has not undermined any of the barn's character and age.

Above: The fire of 1996
ravaged Priors Court Barn.
A firefighter in action can be
made out at the centre of this
photograph. (Tim Wiltshire)

Right: Priors Court Barn's
restored interior. (Author,
with kind permission of Tim
Wiltshire)

Like Brockworth, which today consists largely of an industrial park, Bishop's Cleeve near Cheltenham has also given way to the needs of businesses and commuters by expanding its settlement beyond the realm of its previously rural grounds. This was largely due to the post-war housing boom, growing the village from its nineteenth-century population of a mere 700 into many thousands. As a result, the need to offer its residents facilities beyond those of Cheltenham's also grew.

The local tithe barn stood initially as a reminder of the area's large estate, with acres of land separating Cleeve Hall from the local church and outbuildings. As with many such structures, the barn was built around the fifteenth century to house tithes for the estate, which itself was a summer residence for the Bishop of Worcester. Utilising local Cotswold Stone and timber, likely sourced from the Forest of Dean, the structure stood with the same broad stance as most of its contemporaries.

Fire struck the building during the late nineteenth century, during which it was still largely used for agricultural storage. The entire south portion of the barn was destroyed, worsened still by the disappearance of the ruined stone over time afterwards. By the 1930s the rector, though reluctant to see the end of its use for ecclesiastical purposes, made way for the local villagers who, in the form of trustees, were handed the barn to convert into a village hall in 1953.

By 1956, the south wing had been tidily removed and filled to form a new gable end, and to assist the growing post-war community offered banking services, a doctor's surgery and library within its thick, stone walls. The once-vast interior was partitioned into rooms on the ground floor, with the upper floor hosting a hall fit for dancing, weddings and gatherings, a function often fulfilled by much uglier, hastily-built structures of the time.

At the turn of the millennium, Bishop's Cleeve was serving those commuting to Cheltenham and working at large employers such as General Electric and GCHQ, and the barn now hosts daycare and Zumba classes, in a bid to stay current as the village's primary community hub. In light of its popularity, the decision was made to rebuild the south portion of the barn with the fresh but sensitive approach of architects Quattro Design. The result ensured the barn's continued use as a relevant venue for the 10,000-strong population of today and, when completed in 2014, it married contemporary features such as the elevator, with period farming tools adorning the staircase. In short, despite the huge increase in population and housing, the altering purpose of the village tithe barn has ensured a more balanced community setting for today.

From Cleeve Hill, above Bishop's Cleeve, the Forest of Dean can be easily seen in an arm of Gloucestershire extending down the 'Welsh' side of the River Severn. Wood from there would have almost certainly provided high-quality timber to a number of ancient structures in the Gloucester area, including tithe barns. At Hartpury Court, set away from the linear village of Hartpury, a barn once built for St Peter's Abbey bears some resemblance in style to the one at Frocester. Of particular interest is the roof, largely rebuilt in the nineteenth century when the need to store and thresh crops gave way to pastoral farming, specifically of cattle. It holds two finials, one at either end, depicting its location close to the Welsh border, with one in the shape of an English lion facing Wales, the other a Welsh Dragon facing east into England. Between them is an attractive, patterned, tiled roof that was damaged by gales in the late 1970s before being repaired in 1981. It is similar in appearance to the decaying one at Winterborne Clenston in Dorset (but not as old).

Above and right: Hartpury Tithe Barn features both a patterned roof and distinctive finials. Pictured is the Welsh Dragon, facing England. (Author)

This pattern can be appreciated best from afar as can the development of the farm around the barn to accommodate the milking and rearing of cattle that continues to this day. Inside it is clear that some of the wooden trusses are renewed (estimated to be eighteenth century) and tools to aid cattle farming are still present, such as a tramway built along the feeding passage. A similar set-up exists at nearby Highleadon Court, also built by St Peter's Abbey, though the barn there is not as impressive or intact, nor as accessible.

Three miles north-east of Hartpury's barn is the one at Ashleworth Court, which backs onto the River Severn. Unlike the above examples, this barn was part of the wider operations of the Abbey of St Augustine at Bristol which, in addition to land and estates across Somerset, owned areas along the Severn Valley in Gloucestershire. The barn was built to a seemingly high standard in 1496 under Abbot Newland and was utilised in ways that warranted partitioning of the end bays and, unusually, the dissection of the structure into two distinct barns, each with large wagon porches. Being located so close to the river, the arrival of building material was easier for Ashleworth Court than other more isolated estates and signs that the carpenters responsible for the roof were of reputable quality have been noted by its current owners the National Trust, who were gifted the barn in 1956. Today, one end partition is still used for farming, with the other interior walls removed (one following a storm in 1880). During daylight hours the barn can be viewed at leisure and forms part of a picturesque setting with the main manor house and church behind it.

In Wiltshire, the use of land in recent decades to grow some of its larger towns and develop a significant military presence has seen the demise of some tithe barns. Even in some of the county's smaller settlements, the redundancy of old farm buildings has seen them replaced by housing and other amenities. Wiltshire is partly defined by the recent development of places like Chippenham, Swindon and Corsham, guided by the introduction of military installations, the railways and the M4 motorway. At its southern tip, tithe barns were being removed as early as 1868 when the one at East Knoyle was taken down along with much of the medieval manor that it may have assisted under the Bishop of Winchester.

At the opposite end of the county, the removal of a tithe barn from the remains of Bradenstoke Priory created much debate and concern in the 1920s as it was earmarked to become part of a trend exporting quintessentially British structures to eccentrics in the USA for hopeful commercial gain. Indeed, this was the destiny of the priory's barn which may have been built as early as 1372 along with the priory itself, which had lands extending to its Dorset namesake Burton Bradstock. Businessman-cum-politician William Randolph Hearst sought to add it to his Hearst Castle in San Simeon, California and such was the uproar among Wiltshire locals that the issue even made it as far as parliament in 1929 with Prime Minister Ramsay MacDonald assuring those concerned that the barn's masonry was, in fact, destined for Wales instead. This would turn out to be St Donats, where some stone from the priory was used for restoration. The barn did eventually cross the pond packed into storage units, by which time Hearst had become bored with the idea and so sold it to the family-run Madonna Inn some 50 miles south in San Luis Obispo in the 1950s. Since then the barn has remained in storage.

In 1956, Cherhill's tithe barn from the 1390s was also demolished but had been recorded in paintings and photographs prior to this. It had considerable length and an uneven roof line that had a noticeable 'kink' a third of the way along, just above one of the two large porches that projected from it.

Thankfully, with part of the county in the Cotswolds and others containing affluent rural pockets, many more barns survived the nineteenth and twentieth centuries and have become important landmarks in their respective towns and villages. Tisbury hosts one of the longest in the country (possibly the longest of its type in England) and though now

Tithing Office, Salt Lake City, Utah. While devoid of medieval barns, the USA does have a number of nineteenth- and twentieth-century Tithing Offices linked to the Church of Latter-day Saints. This example no longer exists. (Author's collection)

TITHING-OFFICE.

Old Tithe Barn Cherhill. Near Calne.

Cherhill Tithe Barn. Photographed in 1915, it was demolished in 1956. (Wiltshire & Swindon Archives ref. P17599)

owned by the Fonthill Estate, which had at its centre Fonthill Abbey until it collapsed in 1825, was actually built as part of Shaftesbury Abbey in the fourteenth century, storing produce farmed from the grange that it owned in the village. Before that, there were records of an abbey in Tisbury itself. The barn's grand appearance and subsequent restoration shows that its use was valued by successive owners following the dissolution, and today's display of artistic endeavours inside the vast interior also has great value. Artists exhibiting in what is now the Messums Wiltshire gallery no doubt appreciate having their work featured in a setting that itself has qualities borne of fine craftsmanship in the woodwork and masonry.

Wiltshire's most recognised barn landmark at Bradford-on-Avon is one that is generally known through the nation, even among those not familiar with the tithe or abbey barn concept. Like Tisbury's, it is thought to have been built as part of a grange working for Shaftesbury Abbey as they came to own parts of the town from 1332 and with them, the right to receive tithes. Also, like the barn at Tisbury, it is of considerable length, this time with two large porches as well as other smaller doors and side entrances. English Heritage, the current owners of the Bradford-on-Avon barn, make a point of the lack of ventilation, which often doubled up as vermin control. This, in turn, may have seen it employed for pastoral uses in later life, rather than for threshing or the storing of crops. This differs from Tisbury, where traces of a number of small putlog holes can be seen in the gable ends.

Much is made not only of the size and age of the Braford-on-Avon barn, but also of the restoration process that begun once its farming use had ended in the 1910s. Of concern was the way the roof trusses had spread the walls out over time, despite attempts to keep them in check. Much of the original woodwork was replaced during this time followed by more substantial work in the 1950s. By then, the town had seen much growth through the textile industry as well as both the canal and railway network passing within metres of the grange and barn. Only the town bridge rivals the tithe barn in both importance and age, but Bradford-on-Avon certainly remains a wealthy place for heritage.

This pales into insignificance, however, when compared to the jewel in Wiltshire's crown at Lacock, a village almost entirely owned by the National Trust. As a result of its contemporary use as a period film set, the village receives coach-loads of national and international tourists throughout the year all wanting to capture life defined by buildings dating from between the fourteenth and eighteenth centuries. At the village centre is the tithe barn which, with the presence of Lacock Abbey, is easy to confuse with an abbey barn especially given that the barn is built into the boundary wall of the abbey itself. However, with the inhabitants of Lacock paying rent to the abbey to live there, the barn was in fact used to receive tithes from them rather than to store produce of the abbey grounds.

Its construction in the fourteenth century is largely typical of others with opposing porches and eight bays for storage, but of note is the one gable end that stands at an unusual angle to the length of the barn. The remains of an arched entrance can be seen in this wall, again an unusual feature. The eighteenth century saw the barn used as a market hall after its use storing produce and farm tools waned and eventually it became vacant and was used for village occasions. Given the competition from almost every building in the village, including a much neater but less remarkable barn to its east, it is perhaps surprising to know that this joins the small selection of Grade I listed structures in Lacock.

Bradford-on-Avon Tithe Barn. Photographed between 1900 and 1906, in 1914 it ceased to be part of a working farm. (Wiltshire & Swindon Archives ref. P53173)

Tisbury Tithe Barn. (Messums Wiltshire Ltd)

While nearby Melksham has long since abandoned Lacock's 'old English' aesthetic, its tithe barn is no less fascinating, tucked away from the modernised town centre behind St Michael's Church. It is much shorter in length compared to other Wiltshire examples and hides some of its fifteenth-century origins with extensions and alterations necessitated through its occupation by the local school from 1878. It continued as a school for almost a hundred years, becoming houses in 1974 and now only has the buttresses on its exterior offering any indication of its previous life in agriculture.

Oxfordshire and Buckinghamshire, at the heart of gentrified, rural England, have many relics of past traditions and, often, entities that would otherwise disappear in Britain's more recent towns and villages like family-run butchers, staff-attended petrol pumps and well-established coaching inns, which tend to thrive and flourish.

As a result, a number of tithe barns remain in use in this area and are well-maintained to ensure their survival for future villagers. The National Trust's ownership of Great Coxwell barn, near Swindon, references the importance of allowing these old, vast structures a place in modern village life and thus sees local celebrations, events and the Christmas nativity scene occupy the barn. It is no surprise that this particular barn is so popular, given its size and position in an open field near to Great Coxwell itself. As one of its outlying properties,

Great Coxwell Barn, 1896. The gable end doors were added sometime during or after the eighteenth century to accommodate machinery. (Digital image courtesy of the Getty's Open Content Program)

its allegiance was to Beaulieu Abbey in Hampshire. Interestingly the Cistercian monks were given land at Great Coxwell around the same time that the abbey was formed in *c.* 1204 and the barn was built later, *c.* 1230 (though wood analysis suggests trees were felled for beams as late as 1291). The grange offered immense capacity for farming and, in addition to the livestock and crops that formed considerable wealth for the abbey, fish and honey were also thought to have been harvested. The size and style of the barn is, in areas, quite different from other examples, particularly as it is built on a noticeable slope. Carts duly recognised the one-way system seen in many barns by entering the higher porch before exiting down the slope from the lower end of the barn at the western porch. This porch, too, is somewhat unique in once having a first-floor loft and a granger's office, as well as a doorway offset from the centre. Even after its bequeathing to the National Trust in 1956, the barn still stored hay and farming equipment and, to ensure its use for future generations, the roof was restored in 1961.

Perhaps the most intriguing Oxfordshire example lies a little beyond the ancient Roman town of Dorchester-on-Thames at Drayton St Leonard, where a barn from the fifteenth century was constructed, it is thought, for the monks of Dorchester Abbey. It was known as the Haseley Barn, in recognition of its previous owners, but now it often inherits an uncertain title as a tithe barn under its new owners, the Aston Martin Owners Club. Beyond the attractive weatherboarding, adorned with the Aston Martin emblem, lies a modest but fascinating collection of memorabilia from the marque, including a number of vehicles from the company's past that sit neatly within the barn's six bays. This forms a museum, run by the Aston Martin Heritage Trust, which is open to the public.

A short hop north-east across the arterial M40 takes motorists from 'Oxon' to 'Bucks' past Haddenham, which over time has grown into an expanded commuter village for Aylesbury,

Drayton St Leonard Tithe Barn. (Aston Martin Owners Club)

Notable exhibits at the time of writing are the one-off Aston Martin Twenty Twenty concept (front left) and the world's oldest Aston Martin (rear left). (Aston Martin Heritage Trust)

Oxford and beyond. It is only near the Church of St Mary and its adjacent duck pond that the aesthetic of the village proper has been kept, and behind the church another fifteenth-century weatherboarded barn opens its doors each year for the festive season. The Tythe Barn's proximity to the church and manor house suggests tithes from the manor were stored there and the importance of tithes in Haddenham are noted sometime around the tenth and eleventh centuries. Today, the erection of surrounding agricultural buildings have enclosed the area around one side of the barn, but from Church Lane the barn's size can be admired in full.

A common theme among the present use of former tithe barns is that of weddings and already many examples in this title have proudly established themselves as their area's go-to venue of choice.

At Launton, near Bicester, the Tythe Barn forms the centrepiece of a farm set up to cater for every part of the wedding process to a standard that, arguably, all other such venues should aspire to. This has grown out of a 500-year history of farming overseen by the current custodians, the Deeley family, with Michael Deeley taking on the extensive restoration of the fourteenth- (possibly fifteenth-) century barn in 1997 in order to preserve it for the village. A lot of thought was put into its eventual appearance, and in addition to rebuilding one gable end it involved a careful choice of material for the roof's rethatching after spending so long with a simple tin sheet covering. Planners at Cherwell District Council initially insisted on wheat straw, thought to be the thatch of choice locally, but Deeley successfully argued for the use of Otmoor reed, also a local source of thatch but one that crucially did not require unsightly wire netting to keep it in place.

The Tythe Barn, Launton. Here, the roof is being rethatched. (Deeley Family)

By the turn of the millennium, the potential to use the barn as a wedding venue was realised by son Will and his wife Emma, who began transforming the area around the barn into a setting that could accommodate every facet of the wedding experience without diminishing the barn's rustic qualities. As a result, the reception area welcomes clients with a table, stools and other features recycled from items on the farm such as tractor seats, milk churns and stable doors. Outside, the elongated cow shed, attached in part to the barn, allows guests to mingle over a celebratory drink or share a pizza taken from the wood-fired oven built tastefully into the wall. An intimate courtyard area sees couples wed in front of one of the five sets of doors, overlooked by St Mary's Church which, being located immediately next to the barn, can also be the focal point of the occasion. Alterations to the woodwork, in addition to those thought to have been made in the seventeenth century, have included a bar and toilets at one end, allowing the rest of the barn to host banquet-like tables throughout.

Its farming relevance is not lost on the Deeleys, however, and memories from previous decades recount the ten bays being used predominantly for lambing, but likely threshing and storage prior to that. Its location next to the church, its size and proposed build date of 1370 do rather suggest that tithes may have been stored here over time and certainly in the fourteenth century, Westminster Abbey's almoner received tithes from Launton as well as from parishes within London such as Kensington, Knightsbridge and Paddington.

Above and opposite: The Tythe Barn, Launton is arguably the standard-bearer for barn weddings in Britain. (Emma Deeley/Ilaria Petrucci)

In stark contrast, the village of Merton, just south of Launton, hosts what is sadly a contender for the most unattractive tithe barn left in Britain. On paper, the sixteenth-century limestone barn offers a possible link with the former Eynsham Abbey, but in reality the barn's appearance takes on elements from late twentieth-century housing developments resulting in a seamless integration with the surrounding residential area. The porch has since seen plain boards and square windows incorporated into it, showing nothing of the large doors that would have been there previously, and the dormer windows on the roof add to the uncharacteristic brick chimneys and adjacent garages that totally break any impression that this building was ever a medieval barn. Despite the changes, forming four dwellings named '1-4 Tithe Barn', the building maintains its Grade II listing.

Where Oxfordshire meets the borders of Buckinghamshire and Berkshire near Henley-on-Thames, the large, sometimes palatial, properties often have with them nearby outbuildings. Today, in this wealthy part of Britain, these ancillary structures can house anything from the rarest of sports cars to the sleekest of row boats and, where such properties have a farming history, they can take the form of ageing barns.

Bix, a small settlement above Henley, moved its religious focal point from Bix Gibwen and Bix Brand, which, back in the late thirteenth century, came under the umbrella of Dorchester Abbey. From 1875, it settled on the Gothic, Victorian church of St James at the top of the village. It is thought that common land nearby was shared between up to nine different landowners, each taking turns to farm from it and offer tithes to the rector. The nearest reference to a tithe barn is the Great Tithe Barn at Bix Manor, further south from the church, which in fact consists of two three-bay barns with the original seventeenth-century building gaining an extension some 200 years later. It is particularly noted for its curved queen post trusses, which uphold character following more recent alterations to aid comfort. Another twentieth-century amendment in the form of herringbone brick cladding on its south side actually enhances the exterior of the barn and is mirrored in the floor pattern between a pair of opposing doors. Besides the likelihood of threshing taking place in the barn, little is known about its farming past, which ran up until the 1950s, and the legitimacy of its tithe-related title is similarly unknown.

At Hurley, further east along the River Thames, a confusing array of barns lie nestled within the small riverside settlement, most with religious connections. At Tithecote Manor, listed by Historic England as the Tithe Barn, a large thatched medieval structure provides lucky inhabitants with two separate dwellings that result from the original sixteenth-century barn being altered in the 1900s. This was at one stage part of the wider Hurley Priory, founded in 1086 as part of Westminster Abbey and whose many buildings have since been converted into private homes around the village.

The Priory would have also been responsible for what is now known as the Monk's Barn on the high street, possibly as early as the thirteenth century, which has an appearance more like that of examples in Gloucestershire and the Cotswolds. Its flint and chalk walls create a number of patterned elements on its exterior, which is topped by a tile roof thought to have been redone in the sixteenth century. It is now used as one of two high-profile wedding venues in the village, the other also being the 'Tithe Barn' at the Olde Bell Inn.

The inn itself also exists as a result of Hurley Priory and, as one of the world's oldest inns, has origins as its guest house in the twelfth century. The supposed tithe barn here is perhaps the most dubious in Hurley and, despite the aged beams and weatherboarding,

Monk's Barn, Hurley. (Author)

is the most recent, with its owners claiming sixteenth-century origins. Like the Monk's Barn it is now used for weddings and conferences (being referred to as 'the Conference Centre' by Historic England) along with its contemporary brick-built counterpart next door (confusingly also called 'Tithe Barn'), which hosts accommodation for wedding guests. Proximity to Hurley Manor and its requisition by the United States Office for Strategic Services in 1943 saw the estate and the wooden-clad barn used as part of the effort to communicate with spies in occupied Europe during the Second World War.

The nearby village of Bisham adds a fourth barn to this eclectic pool with the tithe barn at the south-west corner of what was once Bisham Priory, founded in 1337. Besides the fifteenth-century barn, which is now a private dwelling, almost nothing remains of the priory and the site now forms one of three National Sports Centres with Bisham Abbey Manor House sitting at its centre.

Eventually the search for Britain's tithe barns ends up at the nation's capital, and with it the expectation that today's regulation and conformism around the way we pay our taxes somehow extends from a legacy left by tithing. It is quite clear that, like in the Black Country, the advancement of society in London beyond farming saw those at the forefront of trading and industry neglecting the tithe system in the same way emerging technologies attempt to avoid tax today.

By the seventeenth century, so much of the city was dedicated to merchants and to industry that tithes became difficult to reconcile and, though some offered token amounts related to land ownership, the concept of payments in kind was all but redundant in an environment edging further and further from agriculture. Only when tithes began to be paid regularly in cash were any meaningful takings garnered again by the Church. Of course, prior to this, tithes nevertheless played an extremely important role in the upkeep of establishments like Westminster Abbey through its ownership of land and tithe barns beyond the current borders of London.

Despite the fading of tithe payments in this area, what is now Greater London does contain a number of medieval barns where the removal of farming land was not quite as assertive or where heavy industry failed to grip the landscape entirely. Of course some of these would have been built at a time when much more of the capital was open land and they act as a reminder as to how land now forming housing, roads, railways and airports was once used. Indicative of how far from London's centre these examples lie is the fact that three of them sit within short distance of London Underground termini, with the location of a fourth settled almost equidistant from two more.

This fourth example sadly no longer remains in the riverside town of Kingston-upon-Thames which lies between the ends of two District Line branches at Richmond and Wimbledon. Like the notable Clattern Bridge, which does remain, the tithe barn was at the centre of the riotous Shrove Tuesday football matches which saw crowds booting a ball through the town towards one of two goals. Wanting to quash the occasion due to the disruption it caused, in 1841 the local police force assembled constables from London in the barn ready to take on the masses, before deciding against action and instead rejoicing with ale and music. Two years later, for the sum of £160, the barn was sold at auction and subsequently pulled down, with the naming of a modern residential street, Tithe Barn Close, being the only remaining major reference to it.

Further clockwise round London's underground network, the Piccadilly Line now runs to Terminal 5 of Heathrow Airport, where the constant flurry of aircraft pass just south of Harmondsworth, a historic village pinned between the A4 and M4. While the impressive barn here (called the Great Barn and owned by English Heritage) is not thought to be a tithe barn, one is thought to have existed nearby. Instead, the current barn of 1420, built to replace others before it, likely stored produce farmed from the land around it (estimated to be some 236 acres) including barley, oats and wheat for the Bishop of Winchester, prior to the dissolution. Later, the land was mostly split among private owners and even the barn's lease was divided for use by multiple farmers in 1600s. Its survival makes it and its medieval oak construction one of the finest and largest in Britain. Today's Harmondsworth villagers would attest that the barn and nearby pub, houses and corner shop face demolition through plans to build a third runway a Heathrow, though in reality much of these features are saved under revised plans. However, the encroachment of the perimeter fence and outlying facilities that such a major infrastructure development brings will no doubt permanently alter the face of the village.

Here the barn at Harmondsworth is referred to as the 'Gothic Barn'. Its length seems endless. (Author's collection)

No such danger exists around the barn situated near the end of the Bakerloo Line at Harrow where a barn built in 1506 resides within the grounds of Headstone Manor. Like Harmondsworth, this barn was not thought to have stored tithes but, in appearance, it could easily be mistaken for one that did, with two porches protruding from the large wooden-clad structure and a vast tiled roof. It was built by the Archbishop of Canterbury but only lasted forty years under his jurisdiction before being sold off by Henry VIII. While much of the barn was used for storage and threshing, like the example at Maidstone in Kent, it was also used for stables, storing both horses and carriages. Farming was conducted at the manor through to 1928 when the Hall & Sons Dairy moved to nearby Pinner (having started at Headstone in 1894) and associated land was kept for recreation rather than sold off for housing. During the Second World War the barn was used by the Home Guard and as a makeshift theatre for the Holiday-at-Home campaign. Following this the site became part of a heritage centre, eventually renamed the Headstone Manor & Museum.

Similar in stature to Headstone Manor's barn is the one at Upminster, approximately 25 miles east at the other end of the District Line. This fifteenth-century barn, thatched instead of tiled and with only one central porch, is again largely dismissed as a former tithe barn, instead storing produce for Upminster Hall which was under Waltham Abbey until 1540. Records suggest another barn, more likely the tithe barn, was in place on St Mary's Lane but then taken down in the 1860s.

After a succession of private owners, the extant barn was sold in 1927 to the South Essex Brick & Tile Company and, in 1937, again to Hornchurch Urban District Council.

Above and overleaf: Lesnes Abbey Barn, Woolwich was taken down in the early 1900s. Here it is shown in a poor state around 1915. It was built in 1515. (Author's Collection).

The council oversaw the development of the surrounding land and the re-thatching of the roof in 1965 which, at the time, was simply corrugated iron. Sadly, this was lost in a fire in 1973 and was subsequently redone. Upon the creation of Greater London Council, ownership passed to Havering Borough Council, who decided to utilise the barn as a 'Museum of Nostlagia' open on occasion to the public.

8

Tithe Barns Today

After researching, visiting and admiring over a hundred medieval barns in Britain, it is clear to the author that they still play an important part in understanding and appreciating an intriguing facet of the nation's heritage. Where examples remain in ruin, through religious conflict or sheer neglect, they highlight the progression of their area to a new era of Christian history, or how society changed its value on goods and commodities.

Those that survive portray a less troubled past and tell instead of the need to adapt and maintain these ancient buildings. While much of this has resulted in previously public barns becoming the most reclusive of private homes, many have instead flourished with renewed purpose in communities, whether as a wedding venue or a local village shop. In

Long Barn, Kennington (London) once stood parallel with Park Place. It was removed in 1759. (Author's collection)

Though a modern build, this retail lot in Uckfield, East Sussex, has features resembling an old timber barn. (Author)

Chisbury and Midsomer Norton, the church and tithe barn have become one over time; in Northallerton and Cosby produce stored has become produce consumed; and in Nailsea and Melksham, England's children have been taught about their past within a building that has an extensive one of its own.

In places where the physical evidence of the barn has been lost, a ghost-like legacy sometimes continues through street names, pubs and office blocks, as we have seen most notably in Liverpool and Lancashire. Like the Mill Streets and Station Roads of Britain's towns and villages, homage to the tithe barn becomes a frequent feature in the fabric of its settlements.

Surprising still is the impact that the tithe barn has had on the shape of Britain's buildings today. Linden Homes, a prominent housing developer, has begun sale of its properties at the Tithe Barn development near Exeter and in towns such as Uckfield, East Sussex, retail lots have been built in the style of their closest tithe barns. Even in agriculture, hay, corn and livestock still require shelter, ventilation and easy access. Though corrugated iron may have replaced thick masonry, the purpose of a barn is still very much the same.

It is perhaps underestimated just how important the presence of ancient barns has been for Britain's settlements over the last thousand years and their loss has in some cases been totally perplexing and unjustified. The loss of barns in the capital at Kennington, Woolwich and Southall has taken them away from the limelight and it is clear that many elsewhere in the country receive little fanfare or recognition. It is with regret that this title cannot continue to divulge details of those once present in Thurning or Spofforth or the remaining barns at Markse-by-the-Sea and Crosby Garrett among others. Hopefully, though, this overview of these landmarks, the first to be published in over twenty years, may spur readers on to research their local tithe barn, explore those elsewhere and cherish the importance they have had in the great British landscape.

Further Reading

A number of useful sources have been used during research for this title, including the websites of: Historic England, The British Newspaper Archive, and Historic Environment Scotland; Great Barns – www.greatbarns.org.uk – detailing the locations of many medieval barns; Kent Archaeological Society; Agricultural History Review; and the British Library's collection of hard-to-find books, which are made available via their Flickr account. Many of the barns mentioned in this title have their own websites run by charities, trusts and local authorities and these too make for invaluable reading. Other notable sources, such as articles, books and journals, are mentioned throughout this title.

AN OLD TITHE BARN, LACOCK.   B139

Local history archives are vital for finding out more about specific tithe barns. This postcard is of East Street, Lacock in the early 1900s with the tithe barn on the right. (Wiltshire & Swindon Archives ref. P234)

Acknowledgements

The author and publisher would like to thank the following people/organisations for permission to use copyright material in this book: Gordon Poole, The Bazeley Partnership (of Bude, Cornwall), Tim Wiltshire, Lancashire County Council's Red Rose Collections, Poppleton Tithe Barn Trustees, Tom Robbins, Messums Wiltshire Ltd, the Deeley Family, Emma Deeley / Ilaria Petrucci, Thomas Rogers, the Tithe Barn Trust (Landbeach), The Tithe Barn (Cosby) and Wiltshire & Swindon Archives.

Every attempt has been made to seek the permission for copyright material used in this book. However, if we have inadvertently used copyright material without permission/ acknowledgement, we apologise and will make the necessary correction at the first opportunity.

In addition to those above, as author, I would like to thank all of the barn owners and managers that have contributed to this title and for allowing me to visit their cherished buildings. In particular I'd like to thank: The owners of Frocester Estate Barn, Tim Wiltshire, Roger Bastable, Gary Hall, Emma Deeley, Tom Eames, Sarah McNulty and the Colfox Family, Lord Margadale, Ilchester Estates, Sue Grant, Julian Benton, Andrew Oxley at Mercure, Lynne Broadrick at Best Western Hotels & Resorts, the Whittington Heritage Society, the Hundred House Hotel (Shropshire), Norton Park Hotel, B&G MOT Centre (Radcliffe), and Aston Martin Owners Club, as well as Janet, Douglas and Debra of the Nether Poppleton Tithe Barn Trust, Angie and Michael Eavis CBE at the Pilton Barn Trust, Jo and Barbara at Nailsea Tithe Barn, Minette Walters, 'Sue from Beverston', Martin at Mead Barn Cottages, Graham and Martin at Dunster Tithe Barn, Gemma at the Tithe Barn Trust (Landbeach) and all the staff at the Tithe Barn, Cosby.

I'd also like to thank those who have allowed me to use my own photographs of their barns for this title. Such permissions are acknowledged alongside the appropriate images.

Finally thanks to Naomi at the Wiltshire & Swindon Archives for taking the time to dig out some amazing images, Amberley Publishing for allowing to me write about this brilliant subject and Dr James Jones for once again taking the time to read through my ramblings prior to submitting my final manuscript.